Lotus
Emerging

Lotus Emerging

A Personal Journey

by

Jinna van Vliet

Lightworker
Publications

Lotus Emerging
A Personal Journey by Jinna van Vliet

Published by:

Lightworker Publications

www.Lightworker.com

Publisher@Lightworker.com

Lightworker Books, CDs and DVDs can be purchased in retail stores, by telephone at 702-871-3317, or on www.Lightworker.com.

Edited, designed and laid out by Tony Stubbs, www.tjpublish.com

Cover art by Carlos Rubio

Lightworker is a registered trademark of the Lightworker Corp.

Lightworker is a non-profit corporation dedicated to spreading Light through human empowerment.

Printed in the United States of America

Table of Contents

Preface

For many years I have used parts of my life story as an example to clarify the challenges many of us are going through in our daily lives. As far back as I can remember, I had the inner knowing that my main purpose in life was to help others the best way I knew how. In doing so, I found that frequently I was confronted with questions such as, "What's in it for you? What do you want for it? Why are you being so nice? What's your hidden agenda? Why do you pretend to be a Pollyanna?"*

I was puzzled by these reactions and often felt hurt. I couldn't comprehend why these questions were even asked. To me, helping others without any agenda or ulterior motive at all was as natural as living and breathing, and there was no pretending on my part. To do otherwise was an alien feeling and against my very nature. I am only being *who I am*, a minute part of the Oneness of all Beings.

For a long time therefore, I was very reluctant to write this book, even though many friends continued to encourage me to do so. Many who heard my story felt it had helped them with the challenges they had in their lives. Hearing my story gave them the trust and faith to share their own stories, for they realized I could identify with their problems since I had gone through it myself. It is sometimes a lot easier to walk your path when you know of someone who has walked a similar path. It helped them when they heard how I'd dealt with many of my difficult issues such as persecution, abandonment, poverty, and abuse, to name a few.

Finally, after working on myself and gaining the understanding of our human existence, I reached the conclusion that my life is just one of the many unique strands in the fabric

---

* Pollyanna is a character out of a movie who only saw good in other people.

of the Universe. Each experience is already shared with All at the level of mass consciousness. Each choice, each action, affects every part of creation itself and changes the pattern in the tapestry of our very existence.

I do not claim to know all the answers and neither do I 'see' myself as one who has 'made it.' Far from it, for I consider myself to be just one of the eternal travelers and seekers of Universal knowledge. It is the *journey* that creates the interest and the focus, not the elusive *destination* itself. The ultimate destination, as far as I am concerned, has already been achieved and is already within us. The human journey is only a means of remembering how we got there. The only important thing is to understand that we are all ONE, all parts of the One Source of Divine Love and Light who seeks to know itself.

This book is given as a tool for anyone who resonates with it and I hope those who do not leave it in peace for someone else without any judgment.

From my heart to yours,

Jinna

Chapter One

Gathering Clouds

Where to begin is a challenging step when you decide to write a book about your life experiences, and here I am taking these first halting steps. Where to begin opening the doors of rooms that might contain painful memories?

Bracing myself for the inevitable, I begin with that cloudy time in my life where I started to ask the nagging question: "What's wrong with me?"

I look around me and see everything that I have always dreamt of — a home in the affluent suburb of a major city in North America, a caring husband and two beautiful daughters. Enough abundance to purchase whatever I want to lead an easy life, free of any worry about material wealth. Yet, I am like a caged tiger, full of unease and discontent, without knowing why.

"What's wrong with me?"

I have always considered my life to be full of miracles and am constantly grateful in my daily prayers to God. What is wrong with this unhappy, dissatisfied me?

I have a wonderful family of my own, living in a country coveted by every suffering third-world citizen on Earth. Not only do I have a luxurious home but I also have a piece of wooded property on a lake just the way I used to dream about. I have a prestigious job as a schoolteacher, which is, in my case, another miracle. I am surrounded by wonderful co-workers who are my friends and whose friendship I continue to treasure throughout the years. The miracles I thought were just futile dreams have manifested in the most amazing ways. What more could a person wish for?

Why then am I feeling this way?

There's something missing in my life but I don't know what. Of course, we have the same challenges every North American family has today, where both parents work full time and raise two children at the same time. We go through the experiences of driving the girls to all their activities and try to deal with the ups-and-downs of their teenage years. Facing the challenges of keeping a marriage on an even keel, while juggling a job and the responsibilities of running a household, are my daily norm. But even my regular prayers to Mary don't seem to abate the nagging unease I'm feeling.

"What is wrong with this picture?" I keep asking myself.

I chose to be born on a small island off the eastern coast of Sumatra in Indonesia. I was the middle child of a couple whose marital union was like a boat on a stormy sea. We were descendants of Chinese traders who had migrated to this area many years ago. There were no jobs for the younger generation on the island and we ended up moving to the big city of Jakarta, where we lived until our exodus. We were poor then and often relied on my mother's wealthier family members for assistance.

Over time, the political climate became increasingly hostile towards all those of Chinese descent, and random killings and rape drove up the daily fear factor. Thus it was a miracle that I found myself on a boat one day, sailing away to Europe. It was the voyage of my dreams. Since the day I was able to read, my favorite books were of wonderful stories of the foreign people known to us as the 'white people in the West.' The term 'white people' brought a strong sense of longing to me, and a steady stream of imaginary dream scenes filled my younger days. My favorite stories were about the North American Indians. I could not get enough of these novels and would daydream frequently, imagining myself living in a cottage in the woods somewhere in the faraway land of America ... where the buffalo roamed free.

I was raised with a mixture of two ancient Chinese belief systems – Confucianism and Buddhism. I did not know anything about Christianity until a group of well-meaning Protestant church ladies entered my early childhood years. They told my sisters and myself about a God in Heaven who allowed His only son to be tortured on the cross. I could not understand why any loving father would do this to his son. I was afraid of this God and of all the things He could do to people who did not obey Him. I didn't like this story and so dismissed it from my consciousness. Instead I concentrated on the wonderful treats the ladies provided for us every time we showed up at Sunday school. They taught us crafts, fed us cookies and took us on wonderful swimming and picnic trips into the country.

I established a very strong connection to Mary, the Mother of Jesus, once I found out about her, and this connection has sustained me throughout my life. It has brought me peace and comfort during many difficult times in my life, so it was therefore puzzling that I could not find any peace at that period in my life. I became more irritable, unhappy, as the self-imposed stress continued to rise.

The breaking point came suddenly with the news of the sudden death of a close friend who was supposedly in excellent health, yet passed away from a massive heart attack. I was devastated and couldn't understand why this had to happen to him.

I was brought up in the tradition where any show of emotion in the presence of others, especially tears, was considered to be a sign of weakness and shame, and was thus discouraged. It was therefore a shock to my family and myself when I started crying at the funeral. In the midst of my sadness, I began to feel very angry with God for allowing this to happen.

"Why, why do good, healthy people have to die?" I railed.

For days I questioned God, the almighty Creator. "Why are the bad ones allowed to live and hurt others? I don't understand why you are doing this. Are we not your children, loved unconditionally by You, our Creator? Tell me then, why, why are You allowing this. I demand an answer!" (Did I really say that?)

My acquaintance with God was renewed when I entered the girls' school run by the Catholic nuns. I was a lot older then and this time I immediately felt the rightness of it all. It was during this time that I established a very strong connection with Mother Mary. She was the personification of the kind of mother I dreamed about. I felt that she was my perfect advocate who could relay all my wishes to God-the-Father. I was sure that He would listen to her even if He was busy.

I believed in the story of Christ so strongly that I got myself baptized in secret, which caused an uproar in the family. I was the radical one who dared to go against tradition and join the 'White Man's religion.' It was unheard of in those days for a young girl to go against the family elders. I did not know then, but I had begun to learn to put my boundaries down and assert myself. I was puzzled, and wondered why there was not a line behind me waiting to be baptized, especially as the nuns instilled in us that all who were not baptized would burn in Hell.

Not me, I thought. *I'll do everything I can so that I'll never be taken to that hellish fire!*

Storm Front

Then it happened! One morning I found myself at the emergency ward of a hospital near my work place. I had not been feeling well that morning and although I was already at work, I decided to call in sick and go to the Emergency Room to get some pain medicine. For months, I'd been ignoring the chest pains and migraine headaches, but that morning for some unknown reason, I did something about it. It truly transported me into a storm of emotions, for I was diagnosed with a variety of problems, beginning with a silent heart attack, a stress attack, angina, hypertension all the way up to a potential stroke. When informed of my condition, my family doctor immediately ordered me off work indefinitely.

The news threw my family into a spin. They were stunned, for they had not seen it coming … and neither had I. I ended up under the care of a wonderful young cardiologist who was quite frank with me. He told me, "The medical community doesn't really know what illness you and a number of other women have. You're all suffering with the same symptoms. You're all highly stressed professional women, trying to run multiple jobs at the same time – housekeeper, super-mom and a full-time job. I know that the medication I'm prescribing is not very effective for this suburban illness, but I'm experimenting with an alternative. I've prescribed meditation for many of my patients and I suggest you look into it, too."

"Meditation? What on earth does that have to do with my problems?" I asked. Of course, I was familiar with the term and had heard about it but I thought only monks, nuns, and Indian gurus sequestered on top of a mountain actually practiced it. However I had nothing to lose! I decided to try anything to get myself back on my feet, but even in my wildest dreams, I never thought I'd embark on such a strange, mind-boggling journey.

At first, it was very frustrating because I was getting nowhere. I went to every meditation class, from the ones offered by the YMCA to the ones at the Adult Learning Annex. None of them felt right; I just could not get the chatter out of my head nor relax enough to gain any benefit from the exercise.

In the meantime, I looked for books that could give me more information on this unfamiliar practice. My stress level started to increase again, as I began to get more and more frustrated. My family was very supportive but they simply didn't understand what I was trying to do. At that point I was seriously beginning to wonder myself.

The climax came one morning when I was alone in the house, on the verge of losing hope that anything could help me in any way. I was extremely depressed and unable to find any release for the physical pain. I tried the meditation exercises I had learned so far, but with no success. Nothing worked that morning.

I was mentally and emotionally so distraught that I found myself on the floor, screaming and crying out to God. "You're supposed to be the All Knowing One. Well, you can take me now. I don't want to live anymore. My life is useless. I have no purpose. I feel so alone, abandoned, unloved. Why do I have to feel this pain? Take me now! Nobody seems to care. Why is no one helping me through this? Why is a tea-leaf reader who happened to 'read' my cup at a restaurant telling me that my illness is a phantom illness and not real at all? How dare she tell me that when I'm in such physical pain?"

I felt the anger rising within and I lashed out at everything and everyone I could think of. I blamed my boss, my husband, my children and my parents for all my pain. Then I remembered the doctor's warning that I had a very strong potential for a major heart attack or a stroke, and at that particular moment, I didn't care any longer. I truly wished to die. I did not intend to commit suicide but I firmly believed that I could die easily by not wishing to live any more. (Although I didn't know it at the time, I was experiencing what I would come to know as a 'phantom death.')

I cried and screamed, amazed that my eyes could produce that many tears! I felt betrayed and abandoned. The deep sense of loneliness and separation overwhelmed me. I don't know how long I lay there, and part of me was thankful that nobody could see this pathetic blob of misery, curled up on the floor in a fetal position.

In the midst of my anguish, suddenly a blanket of peace descended over me. It was as if a decision had been made, a corner turned, and things were to proceed from that point on. In my ignorance, I assumed that my prayers for death had been answered and I prepared for the worst by calling the minister of our church to ask him to officiate at my funeral. I never understood afterwards why he didn't call me back to find out if I was all right. It was as if the phone call never happened!

Awakening

What happened next was like fast forward on a VCR, for the synchronistic events that unfolded after that morning still fill me with awe to this day.

A number of my friends had been concerned about me and had tried to help in many different ways. One of them went so far as to ask a doctor who was a friend of hers to help me. As the head of a department in the main hospital, he was a very busy man, so I was surprised when he called me early one morning and asked me to meet him after hours at the hospital.

I found out that he had been using hypnotherapy to help some of his patients. "I'm not too sure about being hypnotized," I told him. "I don't think I could ever 'go under' because I'm too much in control of myself." (What an ego statement that was!)

Of course, he laughed and told me, "It's not the kind of hypnosis you see on TV. You would remember everything and be conscious at all times."

Anyway, I agreed to go through with it and found he was right! I could hear him and I could hear myself answering him. I was very relaxed and found that I didn't even want to lift my hand when he asked me to because it felt too heavy somehow. Yet I could hear the cleaning lady vacuuming outside the door.

I did not think that it worked at first and wondered why he was concerned when he found out that I had to drive myself home. Nonetheless I agreed to come for a second session. Again I didn't think that anything happened and that it was not working. I was in for a rude awakening!

A few days after the second session, I was suddenly awakened about three A.M. I didn't know what had woken me up, but found myself sitting up in bed, wondering what was happening to me. My head felt strange, especially the middle of my forehead, my third-eye chakra. (As the result of the classes and the books I had read, I was now familiar with the concept of chakras.) I felt as if something was torn in that spot. To my amazement, I could feel the tear and see the jagged edges of it, as if someone had torn a curtain in two. There was no pain, just an incredible experience of feeling and seeing something that was not visible to the naked eye. I looked in the mirror to see what was going on but, of course, couldn't see any changes in my forehead at all.

I was stunned and didn't know what to make of it. When I told the doctor what had happened, he told me, "Not to worry. It's just your third eye opening. I don't think you need another session after this. However, I'll keep in contact with you. Why don't you join my meditation group?"

In the meantime, I felt lost again, as if someone had just handed me an unfinished piece of something.

Alternate State

The next synchronistic event occurred when a book about a very unusual psychic named Edgar Cayce crossed my path and I became fascinated by his story. I joined his organization, the Association for Research and Enlightenment (ARE). I also joined a local Cayce meditation group. It was a wonderful group of very loving people and they helped me understand many of the spiritual concepts that form the basis of spiritual meditation versus meditation just for relaxation.

For the first time in my life, I began to 'see' that we are here on earth with the purpose of learning life lessons and how to overcome all life's challenges. I understood that I had to take full responsibility for all the decisions I make and all the actions I take during this lifetime. I learned about reincarnation and, although I was not comfortable with the concept of being 'recycled,' I accepted the knowledge. I was puzzled and wondered why we had to go through the karmic wheel over and over again, lifetime after lifetime. I pushed the whole idea to the back of my mind, thinking that I probably would not encounter it again, but ignorance is bliss, as someone once said.

Book after book passed through my hands and I even went to the Cayce meditation camp in Virginia to learn more. There, far away from the distractions of city life, I felt the extraordinary connection with 'psychic phenomena' for the first time.

One sunny morning, we were guided into a very deep meditation in the middle of a sacred wooded area. I remember thinking how absolutely beautiful nature was and was surprised that I could follow the meditation while sitting on a wooden bench outside. Suddenly I heard a plane flying overhead. The sound of the plane was somehow just on the fringes of my awareness and before I knew it, I found myself inside the plane itself! I saw a woman sitting in one of the seats looking out the small window beside her. The shock of what I saw threw me back down into my physical body on the ground. The experience was puzzling and I did not think it to be real.

It can't be real, I thought. *I must have dozed off for a minute.*

Hesitantly I shared the experience with the facilitators when they asked all the participants for input afterwards. They congratulated me and assured me that the experience I had was real and that my consciousness had entered the plane. I was still very skeptical.

After a week in the woods, I was given a ride back to the city. My traveling companion was a Heidi, a very nice lady, and we got to know each other and became close friends. We decided to visit a shopping mall close to the hotel where I was staying before flying home the next day.

What happened next scared the living daylights out of me. We decided to part so we each could browse at our leisure. Heidi dropped me off at the front door of the mall and drove off to park her car.

I walked into the main entrance and FROZE! I could not move! It was bizarre! There were people everywhere, and wave after wave of energy emanating from the crowd swirled around me. It was terrifying. I was plunged into a nightmare! It was as if I was in the middle of a very strange river whose murky waters were rushing around me, a frightened stone statue, in the center of this turbulence. I do not recall how long I was rooted to that spot.

Eventually a far away voice – it sounded like mine – broke my paralyzed state. " Okay, you can do this. Remember what you have learned so far. Now start breathing deeply and regularly. There is nothing to be afraid of. Nothing will hurt you."

I felt like a puppet slowly coming to life as I began breathing. "Move your feet," the voice continued. "Start walking slowly."

I did and slowly walked into one of the stores away from the throng.

Later when I shared my adventure with Heidi, she broke out in peals and peals of laughter. "What did you expect after meditating in the woods for a week? You have been in an alternate state for days. It definitely is your first time, isn't it? You need to adjust your energies every time you do something like this!"

"I wish someone had told me! I thought I was going mad!"

I was relieved at her explanation, and we both chuckled at my ignorance. The whole experience left me with an increased hunger for more. I was insatiable; I couldn't get enough. I searched for more books, magazines, articles, anything about spiritual phenomena. All thoughts of wanting to leave the Earth plane vanished as my interest in the paranormal intensified.

My priority was to heal myself, not only physically but also spiritually, no matter what it cost. My husband was concerned when I insisted on spending a lot of money on spiritual seminars and retreats. To get the extra money for all the classes I intended to take, I made dolls and painted shirts to sell. I even diverted some cash that I had saved for clothes into my special education fund. I felt driven and nothing was more important to me than pursuing the illusive knowledge of the supernatural.

I did not want to become a 'psychic' at all and thought it an absolute joke when my friends told me that I was one. I knew that psychics were people who could tell you your fortune. My friends and I would sometimes go to one for entertainment and would laugh and compare our readings over dinner afterwards. I bought a deck of cards for the fun of it and began to do readings for my friends. I was taken aback when I received positive feedback and they told me that I was getting some accurate readings.

My understanding of the consequences of meditation was still in its infant stages. My experience in Virginia seemed to me just the result of unusual circumstances, because of the people I was with at the time. As far as I was concerned, it could not possibly have happened if I had been alone.

I continued with the Cayce Meditations and tried to get my friends to form a group that would get together on a regular basis. No matter how hard I tried, it did not develop the way I envisioned it. We would meet occasionally and then the group would fall apart. I couldn't understand why this was happening, when I was so enthusiastic about the whole spiritual process. I wanted to share this wonderful knowledge with everyone and was disappointed when the reception was only lukewarm.

During one of the more successful meetings however, we had invited a noted psychic to guide the meditation. She shared with us what she 'saw' that night. She told me, "A huge eagle is hovering above you. You need to acknowledge your psychic gifts. Do you know that you are also a very strong medium?"

Immediately I requested, "Please ask Spirit to take it all back. I don't *want* to become a psychic!"

My request was met with amused laughter from everyone there, but I didn't think it humorous at all. This incident would resurface at a later date and literally hit me in the face. Unable to manifest what I thought I needed to improve my spiritual self, I was at a loss as to what to do next. It was therefore very disturbing when I found myself sliding down into a deep depression, feeling as if I had hit a brick wall once more. This time, I railed at Spirit. "Am I not worthy to gain this knowledge? What's the use if I can't share it with anyone? Am I missing something? Is my understanding flawed?"

With my ego fully intact, I thought I knew for sure what was best for me, and was perplexed that Spirit was not listening to my plans. I wondered, *What is wrong with me?*

Chapter Two

Thunder and Lightning

Although I was more aware of my awakened state, I was still affected by the feeling of failure. I wanted to help God so badly, and get the messages and knowledge across to humanity. In my self-delusion, I thought that I had come across something that was a rarity and that I was part of an elite group.

I knew I was the new kid on the block and needed to interact with like-minded people. I knew I still had much to learn and needed group energy to help me on my way. In my opinion, what had helped me so far could help the other members, as well.

Humbleness and Humility

My resolve to heal became a positive asset, in that it made me examine my motives for wanting to establish a group. I wondered, *Do I really need to be part of a group to promote my own healing?* Myriad self-doubts and questions flooded my thoughts:

Is it selfish on my part? Is my ego that much in control that I dare to consider myself enough of an expert to lead a group? Humility should be part of my personality, so am I not humble enough?

The veils of the past parted yet again and my mother's voice intruded in my thoughts. "Who do you think you are? It's not right that you put yourself first. Be humble. Always put yourself second to other people, especially men. You are to bow down and put yourself down before other people. To do otherwise is shameful, for other people are always better than you are. Always remember that."

When a visitor's voice joined in and said, "Auntie, your daughters are so smart, you must be so proud of them," my mother's answer only emphasized her teachings. "Oh no, no. They are the most stupid girls. Besides, they are ugly and dumb. Your children are so much smarter and more beautiful than mine ever could be."

After her friend left, she turned to me and said, "I hope you were listening, for *that* is how you should answer when people praise you. It is shameful to accept any praise for yourself or your family."

The lesson here, of course, was not only patience with the self but also the notion of self-love and faith. It brought about the deeper and absolute trust to let go and let God do what He had planned for me in the first place. I reasoned, *After all, my Divine Higher self knows what's best for my highest good. But I really need help in the letting go part. This requires true humility, so how am I to do that?*

The Edgar Cayce materials came in handy and I began to use some of the many affirmations he had recommended. My daily mantra was one of my favorites:

"Not my will but Thine, O Lord, be done in me and through me. Let me ever be a channel of blessings, today, now, to those

I contact in every way. Let my going in, my coming out be in accord with that Thou would have me do, and as the call comes, here am I, send me, use me."[1]

At last, the first tendrils of peace entered my heart as the vibration of the affirmation flowed into my being. I prayed for more guidance and asked for the right teachers to come to my aid to help me gain greater understanding of myself. The answer came with an unexpected phone call.

Breakthrough

Judy, a friend, invited me to go to a gathering she had organized to meet Lindsey, a very unusual lady. Lindsey was bringing a message of Love from the Far East, where she and her husband ran a Buddhist center. She also introduced us to Quan Yin, the Goddess of Compassion and Love. I had heard of Quan Yin through my mother and my aunts but somehow had never asked to know more about her. From Lindsey, I learned that Quan Yin embodies the Divine Feminine of Compassion, Fertility and Divine Love. She is the counterpart of the Buddha and is well known in Tibet, China and the Far East. When Lindsey presented me with a picture of Quan Yin, I thought her very beautiful and serene. I understood, of course, that it was only a picture drawn from someone's imagination but it still resonated with me. I felt a connection somehow, as if I knew her and had met her before. I did not understand why she had appeared in my path at that time. I still had a lot to learn about synchronicity!

I had gone to the gathering merely to support Judy with her spiritual journey, but I left with more questions and more thirst for the knowledge Lindsey had brought with her.

I learned a different kind of meditation technique that night and also found out that Lindsey was a very powerful healer. She

[1] From *Search for God* (ARE)

worked with different healing modalities, including Reiki, which I'd never heard of before. I booked a session with her, having no idea what I was in for.

The session was held in Judy's spare bedroom. Lindsey had brought a gift for Judy – a beautiful, translucent white statue of Quan Yin that stood on a table in the room that day.

Lindsey was a very gifted intuitive healing facilitator, and I was amazed to learn that she could 'see' what her clients went through during her healing sessions, although sometimes she was not permitted to 'see.' She told me later that she was very honored to be able to share my journey as she guided me through an unfamiliar healing sequence that required intense and prolonged breathing.

I had no expectations of 'the Breath' and at first felt nothing but dizziness. When Lindsey began talking to me, I found it strange that her voice sounded so far away. I could hear her asking me if my jaw and mouth were tight, and I nodded that they were. I felt as if they were locked. I tried to move them and felt my facial muscles contorting with the effort. I experienced sensations I had never felt before, such as shivers running up and down my body, and cold tingling around my ears and hands. When she asked me to turn over on my side, I thought, *Is it over already? Is this all there is?*

Not so! The breakthrough was unexpected. As I shifted my body, it triggered a shift in awareness and a vivid vision exploded into my mind. I found myself climbing a pink crystal mountain. Sharp shards were cutting into my hands; blood was pouring from all the cuts, yet I felt no physical pain. I was close to the top and saw a strange light there. A voice called to me, but I didn't understand what it said.

Before me was a huge, jagged piece of crystal that I would have to grab if I wanted to reach the peak. I found myself crying, sobbing with fear. "I can't, I can't! It will hurt! I'm afraid."

While I didn't 'hear' the voice, I felt it encouraging me to go on. With a deep breath, I reached up and grabbed the sharp protruding stone and pulled myself up. Blood was everywhere.

Who is crying and moaning like that? I wondered.

Waves of pulsing, glowing reddish pink light were superimposed over the whole scene, as Lindsey's voice gently entered my consciousness. "Jin, it is okay. You are all right now. You are so loved. I am here for you. Release your pain. Let Spirit come to you."

With alarm, I realized that it was *me* who was sobbing uncontrollably. That in itself was very unusual because of my upbringing … yet here I was, a total basket case of tears!

Walking the Path

I came to know that even by reading book after book and attending seminar after seminar, I was still only skimming the surface of true understanding. It would be like learning mathematics or any other subject but never applying it in everyday life. The knowledge would be lost and soon forgotten. I realized that the real work begins only when you begin to *live* the teachings, and the first step is to face your deepest, innermost darkness of fear and anger. In other words, learning how to turn on the tap is the easy part; cleaning out the scum inside the pipe so that cleaner water can flow through is another matter entirely.

This type of intense healing is not for the timid and is difficult to accomplish without the help of a trained healer. It also requires a very strong commitment to continue, regardless how painful the process is. Scrubbing stains and dirt from the skin, no matter how gently done, can leave your skin raw. I was deeply grateful and thankful that Spirit had sent me such a loving healer who I could trust completely.

"Rome was not built in a day," and neither could spiritual advancement be achieved without effort and hard work. Lindsey taught me that we are made up of so many layers and it takes a lot of determination and courage to release all the compacted energies within each layer.

I had a number of sessions and felt like a raw onion after each one. No wonder my physical health was in such poor condition. All my lower bodies were in pain and trauma because of all the negative emotions I had accumulated throughout my lifetime. The first waves of intense releasing energies were targeting the outermost layer – the most recent emotions I had put upon myself. I was determined to release all of it, targeting every layer … or at least as much as I could.

The first thing on the agenda was to realize that I had to learn to love me first. I had no understanding of the energy of 'love.' I wondered, *How can I assume that I'm a loving person, insisting that I love everyone around me if I don't even know how to love myself?* When I saw others putting themselves first, I would think of it as being selfish. Finally the light bulb went on in my brain when I realized there was a huge difference between being selfish and practicing self-love. However, the process of loving oneself was not as easy as I'd thought.

When I began to look inward at the personality within me, I felt embarrassingly childish as I faced myself as the person who donned the victim costume over and over again. *Why is it always me? Nobody loves me! Poor me! Everyone is always blaming me. It's always my fault! Why can't I be pretty and well liked? Why doesn't my boss acknowledge the hard work I do? Why do I always end up getting all the unwanted assignments? Wait until I have the opportunity to hurt them back!*

It began a painful process of self-evaluation. *Where did that revengeful thought originate? Was I really that childishly selfish?* I resolved to take a more critical look at my ego-self. I dug deep and faced the resentments, jealousies, anger and pain. I realized that all the people whom I thought hated me because they were so mean to me were playing the difficult roles I had asked of them. Their actions were meant to push me over the edge, to force me to get up out of my comfort zone. In Spirit form, they loved me so much that they had agreed to play this role, even though they knew that it would be painful to their own Soul to do these negative acts. No one was to blame for all the difficult times I'd had. It was my own attitudes and belief systems that had colored all my reactions and choices in life. It was time for me to take full responsibility for all my choices of thoughts, words and deeds in my life. I wanted to thank many of these helpers for their role but, of course, realized that the veil was as thick for them as it once had been for me, and that they would not understand my gesture of gratitude.

Anger

A number of healers and psychic readers had asked me time and time again why I was so angry and why I did not love myself. My anger and low self-esteem were part of the root causes of all my illnesses. I did not understand what they were trying to tell me because I felt that I was not an angry person. I rarely erupted in anger towards anybody. Had I not shown how I loved everyone by doing everything for them? *I* knew what was best for everybody, and *I* had the right answers for each and everyone. Ego-control was truly deeply entrenched in my mind, and I had certainly buried this dark energy in a deep well within me. But as I continued to face my darker self, all of it exploded out of me repeatedly. I wondered, *Where did all this anger come from?*

I mentioned earlier that when I was young, the situation in Indonesia was getting more violent. My parents decided to make a daring move and, with whatever money they could spare, they sent me and my two younger siblings to my aunt in Singapore. Singapore was still under English dominion at that time, and I lived there for three years.

Layer by layer, the source of my anger was revealed to me. First I was angry towards my parents and family, as I realized that my time in Singapore took away my chance of a higher education. I had to learn English and so was put in a class three years lower than my abilities just because I didn't speak English. There was nothing I could do about it since I was considered a minor. It was in Singapore that I got myself baptized in the Catholic Church. My aunt was so incensed that she almost threw me out on the street.

My next rebellion came when suddenly, out of the blue, the family decided to arrange a marriage for me. I was only seventeen and had never met the young man who was about fifteen years my senior. With my parents' blessing and approval, my cousin, who also lived in Singapore, arranged the marriage contract with the intent to consolidate her business empire with the fortunes of the young man's family. I was furious.

Here was another opportunity to learn how to set my boundaries. I began to fight, using any ammunition I could think of, by vocalizing my opposition. My options were almost non-existent and my only resources were my prayers and calls for help to Mary. My family was not happy with me because, again, it was unheard of for a female child to refuse the 'guidance' of her elders. My reputation as a willful and rebellious child made the rounds of family gossip!

Feeling sorry for myself, I cried out, "Why me? Why is God punishing me? What did I do wrong? What heinous sin have I committed in my past?"

It was many years later that I realized the wisdom of my objections. To this day, many cultures still insist on a family's arranging a daughter's marriage to a man they have never met. Luckily, some unions are successful and the couple learns to love one another. However, a number of the contracts may end up in major abuse and sometimes in the wife's death. I was confronted with one such story during my counseling and healing sessions later on. My heart was filled with deep sadness and compassion when the young woman sobbed in my arms, "I wish I had known your story, Jin. It would have helped me. It would have given me the courage to fight back just like you did."

I told her that somehow back then I realized that looking after myself first was a priority for survival. I wanted to take control of my own life. Unknowingly putting my needs first gave me the strength to stand my ground.

To this day, I am still awed at what happened next. My rescue came in a most unusual manner. The timing was absolutely perfect. Suddenly, war broke out between Indonesia and Singapore. My siblings and I were Indonesian citizens and were immediately ordered out of the country. The British Navy had created a blockade around Singapore with warships, but to leave by air, we had to fly first to a neutral country and then home from there. We had no money to do that, so out of desperation, my aunt became very resourceful. She went to the harbor and paid a local smuggler to get us out.

I remember hunkering down in his small boat, hiding under a canopy with six other people who were in the same situation. We slipped quietly past the huge English warships and out to sea. The smuggler dropped us off on a remote beach of a tiny island that had one village on it. We had to wade through the water onto the beach and then walk through the bush to reach the village without being detected. The next day, we were able to travel to a larger island where we could board a ferry to take us to the main island where Jakarta was located.

We were caught as we entered the town. We had no entry papers and, being of Chinese descent, were immediately put under house arrest at a small inn. The police knew that we had come in from Singapore and accused us of being spies. Every day, a number of us were escorted to the police station and interrogated. I recalled the feeling of a strange silence surrounding me as I sat before them. I was not afraid of these men as I kept repeating, "I am not a spy. I am a citizen who only wants to go home."

Questions flashed across my mind endlessly like a neon advertisement on a billboard: *What have I done to deserve this? What dark, evil thoughts triggered these horrible events in my life? Why am I being punished again?*

Months later, my family and friends were relieved when they found out that I had not been raped. That possibility never entered my mind at all during the whole ordeal. In fact, I was so naïve, I didn't even know what 'rape' meant.

We were finally released with the help of the local Chinese community who knew some of the police officers. It took us six weeks to reach home. Like an erupting volcano, my anger exploded as I confronted my parents. "Why did you do this to me? I don't have any friends any more. My schoolmates are strangers to me now. They have graduated and are beginning their university year. I'm not even a high school graduate."

The green-eyed monsters of jealousy, anger and resentment took residence in me and hid in their lair for the next few years. Although my parents immediately hired the tutors I demanded, I held them responsible for my misfortunes.

Decades later, I did not know I was capable of producing such a deluge of tears, over and over. I began to grasp the idea of forgiveness, especially forgiving myself, and I found that the hardest assignment to complete.

Session after session, I was determined to release all the blockages in my fields. My body felt as if it had gone through a washer wringer and then hung out to dry. It felt as if thunder and lightning were hammering at every wall and door I had built around myself. My thoughts were punctuated with, *Oh My God!* exclamations, as I saw my life through a completely different window during these early stages.

Lindsey and I talked and talked after each session. She told me the Quan Yin statue turned pink when I began my breakthrough, that I am connected to the Goddess, and that it was time for me to wake up to that reality. I realized now the clue that the Goddess and my Higher Self had hidden in my name. Indonesia was a Dutch Colony at the time I was born and so I was registered in the Dutch language as Jinna. My family however pronounced my name as Yin Na.

As my vibration began to change, the visions during sessions changed as well. During one session, I had my first out-of-body experience and found myself floating above my physical body. The most beautiful Angels of Light escorted me to a place of absolute Love and Peace. For the first time in my life, I felt completely loved, unconditionally and compassionately. I felt huge soft wings enfolding me and I came out of the trance state with my arms wide open. Lindsey was often in tears herself as she could witness what I was going through. Our tears were different this time – tears of joy and deep gratitude.

I am forever grateful to her and to this day, she is one of my dearest friends. I had come through the Dark Night of the Soul, bruised but whole again. I realized that I'd already begun to learn how to love myself by focusing on my own healing first. (This reminded me of the instructions a flight attendant gives to passengers, "Always put the oxygen mask over your own face first before you help others.")

I would feel so guilty every time I took time for myself, so to assuage my guilt, I would often increase my efforts to do extra things for my family and friends and, of course, would feel rejected when my efforts were not acknowledged. But I reminded myself, *How can I begin to help others if I have not healed myself?* I stepped up my efforts to do just that. Dinner was often take-out during these times of learning and I insisted on hiring a cleaning lady to help me with the housework.

There, I thought. *I've done it. My life will be much smoother and better now.* But little did I know, I'd only peeled away the first few layers and much more was to come.

Chapter Three

Spiritual Emergency

A sense of calm acceptance settled over me as I continued my journey. I felt I was ready for anything now and was looking forward to the next chapter in my book of spiritual awakening. I should not have been so enthusiastic! As the sayings go: "When the student is ready, the teacher will come," and, of course, "Be careful what you ask for … because you might just get it." A different teacher entered my life soon after.

Out-of-Body

A friend suggested that I attend her meditation circle one evening. I agreed and went with her, not knowing what kind of meditation she was into. I should have known that there were many types of meditation since I experienced a different kind with the ARE group.

I was a bit uneasy when I realized that the session was held in complete darkness. What happened next threw me in a tailspin of confusion. The chair I was sitting on began to shake and move throughout the whole meditation. I was wondering if the building was close to a railway track or if there was a mild earthquake. I did not want to disturb anyone and said nothing until the session was over. I was shocked when I asked if anyone else had felt the tremors and was answered only with laughter. No one else had felt the shaking!

The teacher, I found out, was a Spiritual Minister who trained anyone who wanted to become a psychic. She asked me, "Please come back because I think you have 'the gift.'"

"What gift?" I asked, but she would not elaborate. Instead she turned to my friend and said, "Do you see now what I was talking about last week? Some have it and some are just wannabes."

My friend told me what that was all about. Apparently this particular group had been meeting for a while and one of them felt that she had completed the training. She declared that she was now a psychic and demanded the teacher's verification. The teacher told her, "You do not have the gift and you're just deluding yourself." The student had become angry and left, never to return. I was reluctant and uncomfortable after listening to all the stories, because I still did not want to become a psychic. "You'll never know whether you have the gift or not if you don't come back," my friend argued.

Yes, you guessed it. I went back! Someone should have reminded me of the expression "Curiosity killed the cat!" When I entered the room, I noticed a number of crystals in a strange pattern in the center of the circle. The session started with the teacher telling everyone to move their chairs away from me to give me more space. She never offered an explanation and I was too embarrassed to ask. I should have picked up on the clues! What happened next was like a bizarre film clip out of a horror movie.

I could hear the teacher's voice telling me, "Let go. I will keep you safe."

Safe from what? was my last conscious thought. The supporting group energies were very strong that night. I could still feel my body and hear her voice, yet I also felt myself floating upwards, as if I was swimming in liquid honey. I didn't have the comfortable feeling I'd had when I first left my body during one of my sessions with Lindsey, and was somewhat reluctant to move.

Suddenly, I saw a beautiful angel above me who beckoned me. I swam towards her and was brought to a very beautiful and peaceful place. Suddenly I felt my body jerking and realized that I had no control over my body although I could feel its every movement. My legs were sliding almost out of the chair and my feet were kicking sideways. Then strangest of all, a voice began to speak and I wondered, *Who's talking?* It sounded like me but why was I saying all those things? I could hear my voice speaking in a raspy tone, "This one won't let go completely." The voice had a short conversation with the teacher, whom I then heard telling the voice, "Go away now and return the body to its owner."

Imbalance

I knew the moment I was back in my body because my whole body was shaking and I felt extremely cold, so cold that my teeth were chattering and I was shivering all over. This was not a nice experience at all!

People around me were talking excitedly and asking questions. Later they told me that they had been waiting for this manifestation and that it was not my voice that spoke.

Apparently this group had been working towards achieving mediumship capability. As yet, no one had managed it completely, but here I was doing it in the second class. I was frightened out of my mind and almost ran out of there. The teacher did not offer any explanations except that she wanted me to come back. I refused and, although I did meet with her for a private chat afterwards, I never returned to the group session.

For the next three days, I was off balance and out of my body, shivering with a strange chill. Every healer and friend I tried to call was somehow unavailable. I realized later that I was going through something called a 'spiritual emergency.' I could not concentrate on anything and felt out of focus. I couldn't even walk properly and would stumble into furniture and doorways. Once I was out of the storm, I guessed I had to run through the whole gamut of trials by fire on my own to gain the wisdom of the experience.

Finally Lindsey returned my call and immediately she and other healers worked on me to bring me back into balance. I had my answer but at what cost? At least I decided I did *not* wish to go through that experience again. I'd never wanted to become a psychic reader, remember, let alone a medium!

Chapter Four

The Healer Within

I was very thankful to my friends who came to my rescue. Experiencing different modalities of energy healing on my own body gave me the appreciation of what energy healing could do, and I decided to explore this area of healing further.

First it was Therapeutic Touch and then Healing Touch. Lindsey was one of many psychic friends who told me that I was a healer and that they could see the healing energy in my hands. I had always been interested in herbal medicines and found it humorous when someone would come up and ask me for advice regarding using herbs. They must have sensed something more about what I thought of as just 'a fun thing to do.' That I did not think my friends were serious about what I said showed that my trust and self-worth issues were still 'works in progress.'

New Teachers

When I took the Therapeutic Touch class, I couldn't feel the energy in my hands and did not believe in this ability within me. At least that was until I took a Reiki course from another powerful Spiritual Teacher. I'd gone to see Helga for a psychic reading at first and was quite taken aback when she told me, "When you called for an appointment, my guides told me to expect a very different client, so I was curious about you when you walked in."

She greeted me with, "Oh so it's you!" It made me wonder myself, as I had an immediate rapport with her. She channeled the reading and validated many of the incidents that had influenced my life since my illness. She repeated the message I'd received earlier that I was being groomed and prepared for something. She confirmed that I have the healer's touch and also the psychic channels to become a medium. I remembered the last psychic who told me the same thing, and *still* didn't want to become a psychic. I had enough difficulties dealing with my own challenges, but obviously Spirit had other plans for me and refused to take back the 'gift,' as I was finding out the hard way.

Helga also taught weekly meditation classes and joining the class was by invitation only, so I was surprised when she invited me to join after our first meeting. She later told me, "I can 'see' how far along a person is in their spiritual work, how committed they are and at what stage of development their psychic talents are. Meditation opens the spiritual centers we all have within us. It's a natural process for all of us to develop these gifts. Look at it as music. Everyone knows how to sing a simple song but it takes talent to be able to sing opera."

It was inevitable. I capitulated and gave in. I liked and trusted Helga, and decided to join her class in psychic development. Here I go again – the new recruit – but it was different this time. We would meet in her comfortable living room and the sessions were held in dim light. I greatly enjoyed the classes, the group was friendly and loving. I did not really care about developing anything but I valued the friendships and the sense of camaraderie. I had found my comfortable niche and was looking forward to becoming a permanent participant.

Helga would often call on specific members during a meditation session and asked them to join her energetically in trance state. As a new member, I was therefore surprised when she began to include me in this more advanced group. I took it in stride for a while until one night I asked her about it. She smiled, "I've been watching you. Your field showed me that you are moving by leaps and bounds at a much more accelerated pace than any of the others."

I was not sure how I felt at this unexpected answer.

Reiki energy

Helga also gave Reiki classes. It was not the first time I'd heard about this healing modality and I signed up immediately for all her Reiki tuition.

As I progressed in my training, I began to have more vivid dreams and was startled when I was also given a number of powerful visions. I'd always been afraid of snakes and when I found snakes encircling my arms one night, I woke up screaming, trying to pull off the snakes, but was only able to tear off their flesh. Their scaly skin was left writhing on my arms. I shudder at the memory of it! The nightmare repeated itself during a meditation and left me with chills up my spine. When I asked Helga about the snake dreams, she started laughing. "Think about it, Jin. What symbol does it look like when you see a snake wrapped around a straight object?"

I was stunned! Of course, it was a caduceus, the medical symbol, and the healer's signature!

"Do you accept your destiny? You have a choice," she told me.

I remembered my affirmation: " My will is your will and Divine will is my will." I then understood the meaning of, 'Let go, let God.'

"Spirit knows who you are," she chuckled.

I started my first Reiki class and prepared myself for my first attunement. I immediately entered a trance state and was in the center of a very clear vision. Mary and Jesus were standing before me, and in front of them was a golden basin on a pedestal, filled with an iridescent golden liquid. "Are you ready?" they asked.

"Yes, I am," I replied.

With a shock, I felt the snakes back on my arms. I didn't realize that tears were streaming down my face at that point. I did not try to tear them off my arms like the last time. I did not scream. As soon as I accepted the feel of the scaly snakeskin, the fear slid off me like a soft cloak. At that very instant, the snakes changed into beautiful Chinese dragons with their tiny heads resting on the back of my hands. Mary asked me to put my hands into the bowl and as I did so, the dragons began to drink the golden liquid, emptying the bowl completely. I did not see any physical changes on my arms when I returned but trusted and accepted the vision completely.

A few days later, I went to visit Lindsey to say goodbye as she was on her way back to Malaysia. She had not seen me for a while and I had chills up my spine when she looked at me with a strange expression on her face and blurted out, "Do you know that both of your arms are coated in gold? What have you been up to?"

I smiled; the healer within me had been awakened.

More people came to see me although I did not advertise outside of my immediate circle of friends and family. Every time a client responded with amazement at the result of a treatment, I was filled with humility and awe. I often thought: *How incredibly the Universal Healing Energies work and how sad that not many people believe in it.*

I considered myself only an instrument for the Divine energies and continued to be amazed at what I considered to be miracles. One such incident will be forever etched into my memory. A wonderful lady in her seventies came to me one day. Her doctors had insisted that she needed a leg brace, for she was having difficulty walking and could no longer even walk her dog. I told her, "You are in charge of your own healing and do not expect a miracle pill."

She understood and for the next six months she faithfully arrived in front of my door every week. Then one day I received an excited phone call from her. After I had calmed her down so I could at least understand what she was trying to tell me, she shared the following with me. "I got up this morning and without thinking went downstairs (stairs were not easy for her), got the dog leash and took him for a walk to the river. I didn't realize what I'd done until I got back home just now! I'm walking without any pain!"

She was ecstatic and she never had to wear that leg brace. Such is the power of healing within the human heart!

Chapter Five

Transplanted

Things shifted again for me after that. I offered healing sessions for my friends, which they accepted readily. At first I did not feel right charging anything for my work until I realized that by doing so, I did not honor the work I was doing and also did not allow my clients the opportunity to create an energy exchange for themselves. As for myself, I have always paid whatever fees were asked without question, for I valued the service and honored the facilitator. It was clear to me right away how the energy flowed and I definitely wanted to direct the flow back to myself.

I remember the astonished look on a therapist's face when I insisted on paying her more than she had asked for the session. When I explained the reasons behind my action, she had tears in her eyes. "No one has ever honored me like this. You have no idea what you have done. I'm in dire need of some cash today and the amount you're giving me is *exactly* what I need." God does work in mysterious ways!

Changed Person

In the meantime, my family was still puzzled and uncertain about the changes in me. I sometimes felt as if I was in the deep stillness of the eye of a storm as people's emotions and the power of the winds of change roared around me.

My husband did not know how to handle this change and at one point yelled out in frustration, "I don't know you anymore! Where is my old wife, who I can relate to?"

I asked him, "Do you love me enough to give me the time to continue my spiritual work since it's helping my physical health?" He could see the result of my work, for my health had improved a hundredfold. I was a lot calmer and was not depressed or frustrated any longer. But he was afraid I was being brainwashed by a cult and concerned that I would harm myself. I tried to assure him it was not true. He was very patient with me although he continued being uncomfortable with the whole spiritual scene.

I reentered the workforce after five months of sick leave and realized the difficult challenges I had to face. The 3D world was still very much around me, with all the problems of duality, of the war between Light and Dark. More effort was needed on my part to keep myself centered and peaceful amidst the chaos and challenges of everyday life. I kept my focus on faith and trust in Spirit that whatever happened was for my highest good would occur in its own time. Synchronistic things had already happened in my life and I knew they would continue throughout my life, as long as I allowed the Divine part of me to do her work.

Intuition

To qualify for retirement, a teacher had to meet the '90 factor,' which was age plus years of service. I needed four more years to meet this requirement. Strangely, I was given a much easier assignment than I'd had in years and suddenly the miracle happened again. The rules were unexpectedly changed and the qualifying factor was lowered to 85 years. I was ecstatic, for it meant that I could retire the following year.

I retired in the summer of 1999 and was free to pursue the real work I felt called to do. Once again, a number of intuitive friends had told me I was being groomed for a special job, which included teaching spiritual knowledge and Energy Healing. I did not put much weight on their messages since I still maintained my focus of healing myself. *Besides,* I told myself, *I'm really not qualified to teach anyone about spirituality because I don't know enough about it.*

I had begun receiving intuitive messages and at first it was difficult to trust that quiet voice within. It was more a knowingness than a human voice, and I often questioned the validity of it. I became more aware of it as I continued working on myself, and receiving massages and energy work. I enrolled in different healing modality classes and faithfully continued attending Helga's weekly Developmental Meditation circles.

Often it was not an easy journey. She lived about one hour away and I had to drive on a major highway on my way home at night. There were times when I did not get home until one a.m. and did not know how I even got home. Oddly though, I felt completely safe. I had no fear and could sense a Golden Presence beside me every time.

I felt I needed those classes and was determined to get there whether or not there was a thunderstorm or a snowstorm. I understood that I had to choose what was more important for me and once the choice had been made, it required my full commitment.

The Move

The first messages of more changes came and I knew that I was about to move north, but where exactly, I did not know. I thought perhaps it would be in the area where we had our summer camp in Haliburton, a beautiful spot on a lake in Northern Ontario. However, Spirit had other plans for me.

In November my husband told me that he had applied for a transfer to the North. "Where exactly?" I asked.

"About four hours north of Toronto," he answered.

Not where I thought it would be, but it was north! When I told him I'd start packing, he thought I was being silly. I went with him for his interview a week before Christmas and he was in his new position by January, 2000. I stayed behind to pack and put the house up for sale. When I told him, "Don't worry. The house will be sold in six weeks at the price we want," he was very skeptical and continued to be so until it all came to pass exactly as I knew it would.

It was another strange synchronistic coincidence that connected my husband with the perfect real estate agent, who was very kind and helpful. Through the agent, my husband was able to rent a wonderful cottage right on the shores of a lake just south of the city. He knew I would love it as soon as I saw it and he was right. It was secluded, very quiet, a perfect place for deep meditations and nature walks. The cottage had been empty for quite a while. The owner had no intention of renting it after experiencing major problems with his last tenants. Therefore I considered it another miracle that the landlord immediately agreed to rent it out to us at a very reasonable price. He told us that we could stay as long as we wanted. He was very happy to have us as tenants looking after his property. We lived there for two and a half years. They were the most peaceful years I ever had in my life.

We moved into the cottage fully in summer, 2000, and it was a dramatic change for me. My friends were upset when they found out that I was moving and wondered why I agreed to leave behind everything I had known for 25 years. I didn't know anyone in this new location and yet I didn't feel lonely. I did miss Helga's classes that year but understood that it was the perfect time for me to begin my inner work on my own. I trusted Spirit completely and knew that whatever was in store for me would come to pass in its own synchronistic time. I began to ask for more clarity, knowledge, and wisdom to help others and myself.

Quiet Respite

My daily life underwent a complete makeover. From a very busy and active life, I found myself transplanted to a quiet, almost hidden life. The location of the cottage itself was so secluded that it was not visible from the road, and the driveway to the front door was even hidden by huge old cedars, which I lovingly called 'my guardians.' It was a restful time for me and I decided to continue my spiritual education.

That winter I enrolled myself at the Atlantic University as a long distance student for the Masters Program in Transpersonal Studies. My friends had often suggested I write a book about my life story but I would brush that suggestion aside. There were too many painful memories in my life. I thought that it was my personal story and thus it would not do anyone any good knowing about it! It was therefore a shock when I received my first assignment for the University. It was to write my autobiography! Spirit at work again!

I have fond memories of this time of rest. The mournful sounds of the loons and the chatter of the chipmunks were the healing balm needed to heal my inner self. I finally had time to read all the books piled on my desk. I treasured the much-coveted time to go into undisturbed deeper stillness of the Soul in meditation. I felt like a tired plant that had been transplanted into better soil. One that was placed in the Life-giving sunlight, and at last was being watered and cared for with love.

Being fully retired also gave me the opportunity to attend spiritual seminars that required traveling to more distant locations. The first one that called to me was a weeklong training in Intuition at the ARE Center in Virginia Beach, near the university's headquarters. I had always wanted to visit the ARE center in Virginia Beach, the place where Edgar Cayce began his work. And it gave me the opportunity to meet other ARE members and also to meet with the university's teachers personally. I found out that not only was it an inspiring program but the synchronistic happenings during my stay there were incredible.

Chapter Six

Reincarnation

Synchronicity

I had never been to that part of the country and did not know my way around. Heidi, the wonderful friend I met at the ARE Meditation camp, came to my rescue and offered to look after me since she knew the area well. I did not realize that she lived about three hours away, and was grateful that she took the time and effort to help me out. She picked me up at the airport and then we still had quite a drive to the Virginia Beach area.

To cut down expenses, I had contacted a lady who was renting out rooms for ARE members coming to the area, but when Heidi and I drove to the address, the lady was not home. She was on holiday and had entrusted the whole house to one of her long-term tenants. At first I was concerned to learn that the landlady had completely forgotten about me. The tenant called her, and she said there was one room available for me but only for one night. I had booked myself in for five nights, for it was a weeklong session. The owner admitted her mistake and said that she would try to make other arrangements for me but, in the meantime, she asked that I vacate the room the next day but could leave my luggage in the hallway. Heidi was appalled and drove me around to the nearest hotels and motels, but there were no vacancies anywhere.

I felt strangely calm, not the least bit worried and thought the whole situation was extremely humorous. I told Heidi, "Everything is all right. Spirit will look after me." I dutifully left my suitcase after the first day before going to the workshop and didn't think about it at all for the rest of the day.

My friend Kelly had asked me to connect with her friend Marie who happened to live in Virginia Beach and who was also an ARE member. I called Marie, who was a very friendly lady. She immediately invited me to have dinner with her and her friends that night. "I'll pick you up after the session, Jin," she said. "How would you like to join my friends and I for a spiritual meeting followed by a potluck dinner?"

I replied, "That sounds very interesting. And I'm looking forward to meeting new acquaintances."

Marie introduced me to a number of wonderful people and since I'd shared with her my accommodation problem, she told everyone about it. They all thought that it was an awful situation since I didn't know where I was going to sleep that night. They were surprised that it did not worry me in the least. Suddenly, one of the ladies came over and introduced herself. "Hi, I'm Karina, and up to an hour ago, I'd decided I wasn't coming to this gathering. However I kept getting an intuitive message that I was to come here tonight to meet a new friend. I am to invite her to my home and offer her my spare bedroom. As soon as I saw you, Spirit told me that person is you."

Everyone thought that it was a perfect idea. I was astounded at this new development and all I could think of was, *Holy Goddess. The angels have arranged where I am to sleep tonight!*

The Eye of Ra

The synchronicity did not stop there. Karina drove me to the place where I had left my suitcase and then took me home with her. She was a widow and was one of the Way Showers scheduled to volunteer for the next few days at the seminar that I was attending. As part of being a Way Shower, she and many others had to give the 'novices' – people like me – a short psychic reading. I had given up my time earlier during the day when they ran short of Way Showers and here I was going home with one!

I asked Karina if she would do one for me and she agreed. Her method involved automatic writing and I was curious as to how it would work. I had never observed this modality of channeling before. She began her centering process and then shocked me into uneasiness when she suddenly started crying out loud and sobbing hysterically. She had barely written anything on her notepad. I didn't know what to do! I remembered a friend warning me never to touch a person who was in a psychic trance state, so I waited with apprehension and kept talking to her quietly. "It's okay, Karina. It's okay. You don't have to continue with this. How can I help you?"

It seemed as if she had been sobbing for a long time when she finally stopped and began to calm down. "This has never happened to me," she exclaimed. "I did not expect this. When I asked Spirit to show me your guides, an incredible feeling of sacredness and power overwhelmed me. All I could see was a humongous blue eye looking at me, and a deep voice coming from somewhere that said, "This one has a room full of angels constantly around her. She is one of the chosen ones. The Eye is always upon her. You are to learn from her."

The message left me stunned, flabbergasted and awed. Then Karina sighed, "All I wanted to do was cry and cry when I heard that voice." She gazed at me ruefully, "You don't know who you really are, do you? The Eye of Ra looks down on you. You are in for some major surprises! No wonder I had to offer my home to you."

"No, I don't know," I replied. "And I'm not sure I want to know. It really makes me very uncomfortable and I don't think I am worthy of this."

She laughed helplessly as I insisted, "Maybe you heard wrong. Maybe the voice was talking about you."

How could I feel worthy when my mother's voice continued to invade my thoughts? "Even though she has whiter skin than the others, she is still not pretty enough to get a rich husband. I might have to auction her off in the market."

She was talking about me to my aunts, her sisters, in the kitchen. Skin color was very important to everyone in the community. 'White people' were considered superior both in beauty, intellect and wealth. The darker the skin color, the lower your rank within the human race. Discrimination was rampant and overshadowed the behavior of every walk of life in the country. I could never come to terms with the idea that I was less than another person just because I had a different skin color. My dislike for the D-word had been etched in my memory forever one sunny day. My cousin and I had been walking to school when suddenly a couple of men approached us, taunted us with racial slurs, and began stabbing my cousin with their burning cigarettes. I was walking on the road side of the sidewalk, and so was not as easy a target. Instinctively, I started running and dragged my screaming cousin with me away from this horrible scene.

I was lucky that my skin would not tan as dark as my siblings no matter how long I stayed out in the tropical sun. I was therefore nicknamed "Whitey" and, according to my aunts, had a better chance of obtaining a husband. Many years later, when my mother was in her nineties and she was not as aware any longer, she asked my husband, "Why did you marry her? She's ugly, naughty and would never listen to me." My mother was a very strong catalyst for me.

As it happened, there was another reason for Karina to invite me to stay at her home. Her neighbor, Mona, who was also an ARE member, had recently lost her mate and was having a difficult time dealing with it. When they found out that I was an Energy Healer, Mona asked me to help her. It was a very powerful session and seemed to help her a great deal. Mona told me that her grief had blocked her psychic sight and she had been unable to tap into her deeper intuition. During the treatment, she was suddenly able to receive a message for me and shared it through her cleansing tears. After the healing session, she was more balanced and got herself out of the depression she was in.

I continued with the course for the next few days and someone would always give me a ride back to Karina's when she was busy doing other things. Something else happened during this time period that once more left me reeling with a feeling as if a turbulent emotional wave had crashed over me.

Atlantis

It was lunchtime and I decided not to go to a restaurant but chose instead to go to the beach to sit on the sand. I buried my feet in the sand to help me ground and connect with the Earth. Meditating with 100 other people all intent on stimulating psychic growth can get you off balance very easily. I sat there in the warm sun, watching the tireless movement of the ocean waves and wondered what I was really doing there. Having so adamantly declared that I did not want to become a psychic, here I was learning how to become one. *I started the process with Helga*, I persuaded myself. *I am just continuing the training for my own spiritual growth.*

After a while, I walked back to the center and decided to enter the Meditation Grove, a small, beautiful, tranquil garden with meandering pathways and small waterfalls. As I walked around a corner, I encountered a man with a very strange musical instrument. He was tuning it and asked if I wanted to listen to his practice session since he was getting ready to perform later that day. "I built this instrument myself," he said. "Ancient musical instruments fascinate me and I found a schematic of this one in the Atlantis archives." I was very happy to sit down on a bench beside him and thanked him for asking me. As soon as he started playing, I found myself in a very vivid past-life experience. I knew that I was in Atlantis during the last few days before the major catastrophic earth changes happened.

I was much taller and older, and remembered that I was one of the Elders. I was standing in a circular half open room with marble pillars facing the ocean. Behind me was the same man playing an identical instrument. I recognized him and knew immediately who he was. The haunting music brought a feeling of deep sadness and I started to cry. I knew what was about to happen and an incredibly strong feeling of loss and grief rose within me.

The cadence of the music changed and I found myself back in the garden with quiet tears in my eyes. "Did you like it?" the man asked.

"It is beautiful" I replied, "Thank you so much for this private performance."

I never did ask his name and never saw him again. I often wondered if he really was there that magical afternoon.

It was the first of many past-life experiences I was to awaken to. It left me wondering and I asked myself, *Who am I? What am I doing here? Why did I reincarnate at this time? What's the purpose of reincarnation? Does Atlantis really exist?*

Plato had mentioned it and Edgar Cayce had channeled the existence of it in many of his readings. Some of his followers had recorded Atlantean past lives during regression sessions. I never thought that it could happen to me. What was I doing in Atlantis anyway?

Several past-life memories happened at different times over the next few years. I am including them all in this chapter to present an overview of what reincarnation for me is all about. What I am about to share is my personal interpretation of the information I have on this subject, and my intent is only to brush the surface, to scrape enough as a background for my story.

*K*arma

I came to understand that karma is closely intertwined with the process of reincarnation. The karmic wheel is a type of recording device that downloads all the information of each life that we go through here on earth. Karma keeps track of cause-and-effect like a ledger in an accountant's book. We ourselves are fully responsible for auditing this ledger. To my utmost relief, I found out that there are no punishments. It is impossible for God, as the ultimate Source of Love and Light, to deal with such dark and heavy energies as punishment and judgment. We have to do the work ourselves. We created the ideas of Heaven and Hell in our consciousness to represent the energies of Duality that we are in right now. In other words, Heaven and Hell are right here, right now on Earth and on the surrounding spirit earth plane. It is a choice we make everyday for we were born with the Divine gift of Free Will. Now why would anyone choose to live in a Hell-like environment, you might ask? That is where the deeper understanding of the karmic wheel and reincarnation comes into play. To illustrate, I will use my own journey and hope that it gives some clarity as to your own journey.

It makes sense that we will only be given passage to those past lives that have a significant meaning to our present life. Why would you want to remember things that will not help you in this life? With that in mind, let's return to the scene in Atlantis. Anyone familiar with the works of Plato knows that he was one of the earliest philosophers who mentioned the existence of Atlantis. For many years, I had looked upon the story of Atlantis as a fairy tale. Then I read Edgar Cayce's channeled readings and began to wonder.

Thousands of years ago, large, ancient civilizations existed that were completely obliterated, the most pertinent being Lemuria and Atlantis.

At one point, both existed simultaneously. The Lemurians were highly evolved spiritual beings and had great knowledge and understanding of levels of consciousness. They were the earlier manifestations of Spirit in human form, and chose to ascend during their lifetimes. My connection to Lemuria did not surface until much later along my path, and I will discuss it within that particular time line.

Atlantis on the other hand was extremely advanced and highly evolved, not only spiritually but also technically. The problem occurred when the masses lost track of their connection to the Divine Energies. Technology and physical indulgences became more dominant as time went on. This eventually resulted in the mass consciousness falling into an imbalance of energies, creating mass karma.

We are made of the Earth's energetic matrix and whatever we do will affect the very soil and stone we walk on. The Earth is a sentient living being and, although she supports us in all our excesses, it will eventually cause an overload in her system. Think of it as someone who continues to eat chocolate or sweets in large quantities and continues to indulge in war games of violence. The repercussions to your body will eventually catch up with you.

The changes did not happen overnight but the karmic wheel was positioned on the track of destruction when people did not heed the warnings of their priests and priestesses. We failed to balance the energies back then and so Atlantis disappeared from the face of the Earth, waiting to reappear for another chance. That time is now upon us. Many of us were there then and were given the promise of reincarnating at the proper time to try again. My past life showed me that it was time for me to fulfill that promise. I was a teacher, a priestess, and a healer then and here I am today taking up that same mantle to help the awakening process. As more and more people awaken to the higher spiritual frequencies, it will help to tip the scale towards balancing the karmic ledger of human mass consciousness.

Past Life Connections

As I understand the workings of the Karmic Board, souls usually reincarnate again and again in the same family circle. With this in mind, I realized that I have been with the same members of my family for many cycles.

The next lifetime I needed to remember was in ancient Egypt. Again I was a high priestess in the Healing Pyramid and I saw myself helping an injured man lying before me on a marble table. Beside me was a young girl who was my assistant, and I immediately recognized her as my youngest daughter in this lifetime. I loved her dearly and on my deathbed I asked her to reincarnate as my daughter in the future.

Her birth in this lifetime was another miracle. The doctor told me that I could not have children and was astonished when I got pregnant with my first daughter. He was ready to schedule me for a hysterectomy when I told him I was pregnant again. He did not believe me at first until he had examined me thoroughly. He told me after she was born that he did not know how that baby survived in my uterus.

I knew immediately that both my daughters were advanced souls who chose me to become their mother in this life to help them with their life lessons. My youngest, however, had that instantaneous, close connection with me. As she grew older, she asked to join me in my healing classes and has accompanied me in many of my spiritual retreats and seminars. She has kept her word!

My oldest daughter, on the other hand, chose a different path after she left home. It took every part of acquired wisdom I had to stand back and only send her all my love. It is never easy for any parent, especially a mother, to release a child, knowing what a challenging path she has chosen. Parents facing the same dilemma would be familiar with the phrase 'tough love.' In my wildest dreams, I did not think that I would have to implement this, as painful as it was.

I was denied the recovery of the past life I had with her, and I accepted that she chose me only to hold the light for her in this lifetime. Any other effort on my part would be interfering with her lesson plan that she scripted for herself. Imagine doing your child's homework all the time. How could she pass her test or even graduate to a higher grade? How could a baby learn to walk if you carried it all the time out of fear that it might fall and hurt itself? I had no intention of messing up her karmic ledger.

Shaman

The most profound resurfacing of memories were those of my numerous lives as a North American Indian shaman.

My discoveries of these past connections gave me the understanding of my fascination with Indians, teepees, serene forests and the sound of drums. Recall how I felt completely at home in the northern woods, and did not realize the strong bonds I had with the land.

My husband joined me in my interest in First Nation ceremonies and rituals, and he came home one day to tell me about a sweat lodge ceremony to be held by a local shaman. It piqued our interest and we decided that he would go on his own first to find out what it was all about. He liked his first experience but kept telling me that I really should contact Lakotahwin, the shaman, myself.

"She talks like you," he insisted. "I told her that you talk about the same things."

I was intrigued and arranged for another sweat lodge ceremony for three of my friends and myself. I was the designated driver and, as it happened, was the last one to enter the house. I was thrown into another past-life scenario as Lakotahwin exclaimed, "Where have you been? What took you so long?"

We were both teary eyed as we hugged. Scenes flashed through my mind of wood fires in a teepee with both of us sitting on the ground sharing our knowledge of healing and spirit connection. She told me later that she had asked Spirit for help because she had noticed changes in the sweat lodge energies and didn't know what to make of it. Spirit told her, "She will come."

The minute I stepped into her home, she recognized me although I hadn't incarnated as a Native American this time.

She began to reintroduce me to the sacred ceremonies and, to my amazement, they sounded very familiar to me. "We're back together again, sister," she said happily. "Our work has just begun."

She was right, for we have been teaching and traveling together since that memorable day.

One other lifetime that resurfaced was a profound encounter that happened after I had met Lakotahwin. She and I were both at a weeklong spiritual seminar and were part of a ceremony of intense sharing of love and compassion. One of the men seemed to have difficulty connecting with me and it puzzled me. I sent him as much light, love and compassion as I had for everyone else in the room and left it at that.

I had my eyes closed during the ceremony and suddenly I felt his presence as he touched me lightly on the heart. Gently he whispered in my ear, "I now know who you are." As had happened before, his touch and his words were the key that opened that past for me. I saw myself sitting before an outdoor campfire this time. In a circle beside me were a number of young Indian braves listening to what I had to say. In the shadows behind me, I could see white teepees of a small Indian village. Softly in the distance, I could hear someone chanting, accompanied by the hypnotic sounds of a drumbeat.

Tears clouded my vision as I opened my eyes. I looked around for him and noticed that he had moved away from me. I went to tap him on his shoulder. "You were the young brave always asking the questions, weren't you?" I chuckled.

It was heartwarming to see this grown man tip his head like a young embarrassed teen as he grinned impishly and said, "Yes, I was." Then he frowned and added, "I did everything you taught me and followed your teachings. Why did you leave us so soon and so suddenly? Why did you leave me?"

I sensed his pain and gently replied, "I loved you all and it was time to leave to allow you to grow and live the teachings on your own."

Oftentimes, I do not know what my answers 'should be' when someone asks me a question. Instead, the words just flow out of me the instant a response is required. It frequently unnerves me and I wonder, *Where did that come from?*

For me, each encounter with a past life memory was as if I had woven another strand into the beautiful tapestry of my life. Each brought me the wisdom and knowledge I needed at exactly the right moment. Each gave me the opportunity to clear my karmic ledger that needed to be balanced through forgiveness, compassion and unconditional love.

Chapter Seven

Circles of Light

When I got home from Virginia, I felt different, a little out of sorts, but dismissed the feeling, thinking that it was just tiredness from the journey. As a welcome home gift, my husband surprised me by having my name painted on the car door. It was very touching and lifted up my spirits.

The First Circle

I had an appointment for a chiropractic adjustment in town and made my first contact with my new community at that time. Two women were in charge of the office, and I came to know both of them quite well. We chatted and exchanged stories every time I went for a treatment. Petra, one of the pair, became very interested when she found out that I had guided meditation circles. She began to ask a lot of questions and finally asked if I would consider guiding a meditation session for her and her sister.

I agreed and the first meditation group I called Light Circle was formed in the cottage. As we came to know each other better, Petra told me that she 'saw and felt' my presence the very first time I entered the office. I knew then that she was highly intuitive and was very honored that she had asked me to guide her.

Things cascaded from that first meditation session into numerous gatherings. Petra began to tell her friends about me and they came to join the meditation circle every week. To this day, I marvel at the fact that they found me, even though I was hidden in such a secluded spot. They came and didn't mind having to crowd into a small space in the cottage.

Abuse

The members of this circle were searching for guidance and were ready to heal themselves. I am still awed at the willingness of each one of them to lie on my healing table and release all the compacted energies they had carried for so long. Tears still cloud my eyes at the memory of the brave and courageous decisions these women had to make. A number of them had to face their husband's control issues when they got home. One spouse ordered his wife never to associate with me again and she had to choose which path to take. All of them opened themselves completely and for the first time I was confronted with major abuse issues that also brought my own dark past to the surface.

My mother was the youngest daughter with about eight brothers and one older sister. Her father died when she was six years old and her mother, her brothers and sister spoiled her. My grandmother and my aunt helped with all her children as we came along. I was number four and my parent's marriage, rocky to begin with, reached another crisis when I was born. My mother admitted that she threw me at my father's feet in a fit of temper when I was only a few months old. My mother could not handle her responsibilities as a parent and I realized at a very young age that she was child-like herself. She was a child who never grew up, as was my father also.

My mother would relentlessly tell anyone who wanted to hear what a difficult child I was. Out of the four daughters, I was the only one who received corporal punishment. It didn't matter who was at fault when my sisters and I fought; I was the only one who received the 'broom' or the slap. The 'broom' was made out of the thin flexible spine of a coconut tree leaf. When you use it to beat a carpet, it flexes like a whip. When I was 16, my mother went into a rage because I did not obey her. I knew in my heart that what she had asked me to do was not right, so I refused to do it. I was lying on my side in the bed reading a book when she came storming in. I did not move, and didn't even look up as she proceeded to use the broom. She kept hitting my legs until they began to bleed. At that point, my cousin came running in, yelling at the top of her lungs, "Auntie, stop. For God's sake, STOP beating her. You don't know anymore what you're doing!" With that, she grabbed my mother's arm and dragged her out of the room. Afterwards, my mother pretended as if nothing had happened.

I thought that I'd finished with releasing many of my dark issues when I was working with Lindsey, but I realized it was far from over, and that I was still peeling the huge onion. After releasing one layer, I needed to face the next one, and the next, and the next. There was so much more for me to study. I forgave my mother then and understood her role as a major catalyst to move me into the life lessons I needed to learn. I had deep compassion for those who were taking the first steps towards forgiving their abusers, for it's not an easy task.

I enjoyed guiding the women's meditation group, and we would extend the time together with spiritual discussions. I found myself sliding into a teaching mode before I knew it. It was truly a test of trusting myself. I said, "I don't know much but I'm willing to share whatever I have learned." I was truly humbled at the show of trust that these beautiful souls had in me. The problem was recognizing the role that Spirit had presented to me and having enough faith in myself to do a good job.

The Second Circle

The second light circle came to me during this same time period. I was planning to attend a Tobias seminar (Crimsoncircle.com) in another town I had never visited. The organizers told me that there were other ladies going to the same seminar and gave me a number to call so that we could car-pool. I called and they graciously agreed to take me on as a passenger. There were three of them and they told me they had been meeting for a number of years studying and learning together. They found that they were at an impasse, and were hoping for someone with new knowledge to join their spiritual journey. Lo and behold, there I was, knocking on the door! They discovered that I had just moved into the area and asked me to talk about my spiritual experiences.

After the seminar, they asked me to join their circle, which I did. My new teaching career had begun in earnest, although my issues with trust and self-worth continued to be a struggle within me. Teaching had always been my passion and it finally dawned on me that my former teaching career had just been training for the role I now occupied.

Both groups of women had many questions for me every time we got together. It was heartwarming to see their enthusiasm and their willingness to learn all about the new energies and the changes that were forthcoming. Incorporating the teachings into their daily lives was not easy and presented a number of them with many challenges and major changes to their lives, not all comfortable ones.

When they asked me to share my story with them, I found there were parts in my tale they could relate to, and it helped them see their own lives from a different angle. Besides serious discussions and releasing of many tears, there were also moments of happy laughter and feelings of sisterhood as we shared tea and snacks.

Many of the new concepts were not always immediately understood and often caused heated discussions or uncontrollable laughter. One such occasion was the gift of a group of angelic helpers, coined 'Runners.' The idea was that they would run and help us with our journey when we asked them to. One lady could not understand why it was not working for her. I asked what she meant and she explained that she had ordered Angel Number One to look after her mother, then Angel Number Two to look after her son and so on, until she ran out of angels. We all laughed together, once we explained to her that you cannot order angels around like you would an employee.

It is so easy to portray angels as having human attributes and to want them to behave according to human values. It's a lot harder to see them as the light beings they are, and to accept that they can help energetically but ultimately, it's the human who has to do the work. Humans are the dreamers and the imaginative creators. Angels are only here to help connect the golden strands of our creations to manifest our potentials.

Abundance

Another difficult concept is that there is enough abundance for everyone on Earth. And invariably, people assume abundance is all about money. I tried to explain that the concept of abundance is about understanding the flow of energy. Money is just energy; it doesn't have any power unless you insist on giving it power. Energy flows like water and needs to keep moving to keep itself fresh and abundant. A stagnant pool is an invitation for scum to grow. The same principle goes for any kind of abundance. It has to flow.

To stimulate a deeper understanding of the concept, I introduced them to the idea of an abundance box, something visual to relate to. It's a small wooden box that can be decorated and filled with whatever abundance you choose to have. I realized I needed more practice in getting the idea across when one person immediately put a picture of a cruise liner in it and another put in a photo of a new car. Another asked, "When can I graduate to a much bigger box?"

The premise is that any coins you put into the box can't stay there for long. I encouraged them to find ways to keep the energy flowing. I didn't ask for any fees for the meditation circle but asked that they put a donation into my box as part of the exercise. I explained that I would take the money out every week and use it to buy the weekly snacks or sometimes donate it to a worthy cause. I told them, "My box always has coins in it because I put more in any time I have some extra change in my purse."

I was fascinated to observe the level of understanding of each person who received this knowledge. After one of my workshops, one woman put in a large bill into the donation box. I discreetly asked her if she needed any change. Her answer still brings joy and deep gratitude within my heart. "What I have put in there is not for your benefit but for mine. I know that energy will loop back to me and what I learned today was worth more to me than the money I put in your box."

She had understood the concept at a higher level. I honored any donation, regardless of the amount, and kept repeating,

"It's not about the monetary value." It was the understanding of the phrase, "Do you control money or does money control you?" that carried the true value.

When the angelic guides and helpers were asked about the money energy, their answer was very interesting. They used our human words to describe how they felt about it. "When humans allow money energy to control them, it creates a strong body odor in their energetic field. To us it smells very bad, like a sewer. It is very uncomfortable for us, so we withdraw from that energy to a safe distance."

To provide the group members with more examples to learn from, I shared with them my feelings of gratitude and honor to the healers who worked on me. I mentioned earlier that I had given more than what had been requested. A year or two later, as I was leaving a client after a healing session, she handed me a $100 bill – a lot more than my fee schedule. Tears of gratitude filmed my eyes when she said, "Don't you dare give me any change back. Every time you take another course, I get the benefit of it and I want to keep it that way. I know that you are about to take another one."

I also suggested that abundance could come in many different wrappings. I encouraged everyone to get very creative and write other things on pieces of paper, for example, "Abundance of peace, ease and grace for the next challenge, patience, compassion, and health," to name a few. Once they understood the concept, the results were amazing. Following are some of the resulting stories of this exercise.

Gloria told me, "I was discussing the idea of an abundance box with my friend, Fiona. Fiona told me that she had just noticed an extra $5 in her wallet and wondered if she should put it in her abundance box. Soon after, the doorbell rang, and at the door was a young boy selling cookies for five dollars a box. With a sigh, Fiona handed him the money and said, 'I don't really need more cookies but here you go.' When Fiona told me what she had done, I saw my opportunity and said, 'Why didn't you tell me it was a small boy? Call him back and I'll buy another box from him.' Fiona opened the door again to call out to the boy, but to her astonishment there was no one on the street. We were both puzzled."

What they did not realize was that they had just been gifted not only with cookies but also with the abundance of a magical moment.

My last contribution for this topic was just as bizarre. My husband, my daughter and I were on our way home from Toronto and decided to stop for dinner. In the restaurant, another couple with two children were seated beside us. As usual, no one paid too much attention to other patrons in a restaurant. We did notice that the family left before we did. Imagine our reaction when my husband asked for our bill and the waiter told us that the gentleman who'd been beside us had already paid it. My daughter volunteered to run out of the restaurant to see if she could find him. There was no sign of the family anywhere! We had been gifted with an abundance of a free meal!

Sadly, I had to close the first circle after only a few months because the road conditions to the cottage were treacherous in the winter and many did not have four-wheel drive cars. I told them that we would continue as soon as I had my own home. I left the second circle when I realized that they needed time to absorb and process the information in their own way. It was also time for me to redirect my energies and attention to finding my own home.

It was interesting to notice that at first, only two from both circles came to form the third Light Circle at my new home. It was a choice everyone had to make to know whether they were ready to make the commitment to walk the path or not. Every choice, it does not matter what it is, will always be honored by

Spirit. In the Eye of All That Is, there are no wrong or right choices. It just IS. There was no judgment and never could be on my part, and I hoped that it would be the same for anyone who claimed to be a Lightworker, as well.

Choosing to walk the path of enlightenment is not an easy one and it requires a lot of effort. It takes its toll at every level of your being – physically, emotionally, mentally and spiritually. Everyone has a choice to walk the road with ease and grace, or to wander along facing each drama and challenge on the way. Once you are well on your journey, it will be almost impossible to return to your old self. You are changed forever!

Chapter Eight

The New Energy

The first Kryon book came in my mailbox during my stay at the cottage. My sister had read the book and thought that it might interest me. Kryon is an angelic entity, channeled through Lee Carroll, who has come to teach us about the changes that are happening on earth.

The Great Shift

I could not put the book down and the material threw me into the next phase of my journey. What I was learning filled me with exhilaration, joy and feelings of being truly blessed to be alive! I bought all the other books in the series and began to connect with the Kryon website. Finally, I understood what the Harmonic Convergence had been all about.

For a very long time, the angelic realms have been measuring the level of human mass consciousness at regular intervals. It appeared that the Harmonic Convergence was one such measuring event and, to everyone's surprise, our level of consciousness had risen enough to trigger the next phase of evolution. The New Energies – at least new to us – were then able to come in, bringing the possibility of raising the vibration of Mother Earth and all her occupants.

For centuries, only a few individuals had been able to achieve ascension by transcending their individual consciousness through sacrifice and hard work. These were the sages, the ascended masters and the saints. The Harmonic Convergence was the expression of the decision of the masses to initiate that same rise in consciousness. The process of achieving enlightenment *en masse* was now possible for all of humanity. The term 'ascension' elicited a wave of controversial debates when it was first mentioned as a possibility for all of humanity. As far as I was concerned, it was just a case of the interpretation of semantics. Personally, I liked the idea of the chance for many of us to evolve and grow into higher vibrational beings while still in human form in this lifetime.

There was considerable excitement in the angelic realms at the news. Everything was affected and by that, I mean the whole Universe itself was facing major structural changes. The whole interdimensional configuration of creation was shifting and changing, as we were moving from the denser three-dimensional levels to the higher vibrations of the four-dimensions and beyond.

Earth had graduated and was about to move into the higher frequencies of the Universe. Gaia, the Earth Mother, was finally about to join her other sisters in the heavens of the higher realms. This is now known as the Great Shift in Consciousness.

Many potential strands of awakening were activated at that very moment of Harmonic Convergence, including my own. At last I had a glimpse of the answer to my question, "What is wrong with me?"

I gained more knowledge about the New Energy and the Great Shift through many sources such as the Tobias Crimson Circle and The Lightworker Group. They were all on the same wavelength and I resonated with all of them. As I explored all the information given through each channel, I felt an incredible surge of excitement and began to devour the material ravenously. I felt more driven than before, and couldn't get enough. It was an insatiable hunger that was not to be filled soon. I went to as many seminars as I could afford, feeling that each offered the material with a different flavor and would broaden and enhance my perspective.

The concept of the new energies continued to fascinate me. As I learned to work with it more and more, I noticed that it had a strong influence on my energetic field. I was starting to vibrate at a much more rapid pace. As I continued to study the material, I was amazed at the speed at which I seemed to understand it. I felt as if someone had opened my head, poured liquid knowledge into it, and my brain absorbed it like a sponge. One of my friends, who had the gift of sight, later told me that she had witnessed this phenomenon during a deep meditation session she attended. She saw it happen to a woman sitting across from her. "The Spirits really opened her head, Jin, and I saw them pour sparkling golden liquid of light into her head. They must be doing the same thing to you!"

I could not accept this explanation in regards to myself for I still thought myself unworthy of such a grand gift of Spirit. The layer of unworthiness was firmly entrenched within me.

The wheels of past indoctrinations were turning, taunting my mind. "Don't you dare embarrass the family? Don't be the cause of us all losing face because of your pride. Immediately contradict anything that would make you seem better than anyone else. Only rich and beautiful people are worthy of receiving grand gifts. Always share with others and donate to charities regularly to ensure your salvation. Humility and acquiescence are the only acceptable behavior patterns in accordance with our ancestral teachings."

Ego Layers

Not surprisingly, Ego was a big hurdle for me. I was continually afraid that my ego would rear its ugly head and block my spiritual advancement, so for years, I tried hard to suppress this part of me. I would not and could not allow myself to be blocked after all the hard work, effort and commitment I had invested in my journey. I could not jeopardize the precious knowledge I had gained so far. Therefore I tried to minimize and neutralize every accolade that was sent my way and suppressed the small voice that whispered, "Can't you see that it could be you?" I could not accept that.

By this time I understood the immediate dangers of the Spiritual Ego. It was the most elusive layer of the ego, tricky to admit even to its presence. As my spiritual knowledge increased, so did the tendency to submit to the temptations of the Spiritual Ego. I had witnessed many lightworkers around me who capitulated because they did not understand the implications of this ego state. I recognized this rocky part in my path and asked for help in dealing with this part of myself.

Spirit stepped in again in a marvelous way. I was working on my university assignments in conjunction with everything that had been happening in the cottage during the two and half years that we lived there. I shook my head in wonder as one of my assignments came in – write an essay on EGO!

As I said earlier, I considered having ego to be putting the "I" before all accomplishments and being a kind of egotistical show off, a know-it-all. Going in the opposite direction, such as putting oneself down, showing humility and low self-esteem, would therefore be okay and would not be considered part of the ego. I did not think that having a case of severe low self-esteem was a good thing to have, but having it in moderation was, in my view, not such a bad thing. I was still trying to keep the tradition going of honoring the ancestral teachings and customs. I had to change my thinking on that view and completing the assignment gave me the clarity to readjust my perceptions on ancient customs.

Becoming a No-Body

My assignment was to discuss a comment made by John Engler, a well-known philosopher. He stated: "You have to be somebody before you can be nobody." I was frustrated for I did not know what he meant by his remark. For days I pondered the phrase and then suddenly a big 'Aha moment' of insight flashed across my thoughts.

The following paragraphs are a quick overview of what I learned through my research into this topic.

The Ego is a vital part of the human consciousness and can never be killed or separated. It would be like cutting off my own leg if I were to try to eliminate the Ego. I had to reach the realization of the Self by becoming 'somebody' through the strength provided by the Ego. This ego-strength, this self-confidence is the connection that allows me to tolerate the turbulent human emotions and the constant stream of thought patterns. Without it, I would be overwhelmed and unable to deal with the chaotic emotional input. I understood that I could not stop the flow of thoughts; however ego-strength is the ability to choose which thought remains and takes residence in my mind.

Pursuing deep meditation practices in order to solve my daily problems does not work unless I become a 'somebody' who pays attention to 'all' experiences, not just spiritual ones.

Trying to cut corners and avoid facing all parts of myself, I cannot see through the illusion of the self, and thus true spiritual growth is hampered. It is essential to gain deeper understanding of my relationship to others and the illusionary sense of separateness in order to achieve Ego Strength.

Here was another lightbulb moment! Finally I understood why I frequently felt stuck during various stages of my journey.

The ultimate goal then is not to disregard nor deny the Ego completely but somehow to work towards becoming a spiritual being with a healthy and balanced ego in place. Achieving this higher platform requires 'ego-esteem, ego-strength,' which will grow into ego transcendence. The Ego does not disappear but the highly developed sense of 'self,' when used well, is transformed with the realization of 'Egoless-ness,' or a 'Nobody' state. The Dalai Lama understood this concept well for he said, "*I both am and am not.*"

Putting oneself down, or showing false humility, is the negative side of the Ego and is just as disruptive as the positive side. It shows the lack of "ego strength" and therefore shows a very weak realization of the Self. As we move into the higher states of development, our perception of Self changes. We realize our deep sense of connection with the universe, other people and all of nature. We 'see' that we are just as worthy and just as important a piece of the whole, the Oneness of all things. It will take some work to undo the conditioning that we all have been subjected to in our stages of development in this lifetime. Now we need to replace the old programming with the new awareness that each person is an important part of a WHOLE. I think about it as one huge puzzle with many living pieces and, as each piece finds its spot, the picture on the puzzle becomes clearer and more vibrant. With this visualization in mind, it is easier to accept that every individual is a unique piece, and that without this piece, the puzzle cannot be completed.

The most inspiring example of one who achieved the Egoless State is, in my opinion, Mother Teresa. I remembered reading an article that recounted her conversation with a bishop behind the scenes before she would be introduced on stage at one of her public appearances.

"Mother, how do you do this?" the bishop asked.

"Do what, my friend?"

"Face the celebrity status, the public acknowledgements, the praises, while at the same time maintaining your serenity and humbleness in the eyes of God?"

"It is very easy really. Before I face the public, I pray to God to make me invisible and to allow only his countenance to shine forth through me."

It was noted later that the cameraman who recorded the session was baffled. No matter how hard he tried, somehow Mother Teresa's face was continually out of focus.

Yogi Mata Amritanandamayi once said, *"When you go beyond ego, you become an offering to the world."*

Although my confidence and faith in myself still had its shaky moments, I was more at peace with it now. My fear of Ego had been diminished with the in-depth understanding of its role. I was slowly learning to acknowledge my own uniqueness and accept praise gracefully.

I realized as well that within the constant changes of the new energies, there was no room for a heavy, unrealized Ego. Part of the awakening process was to become aware and recognize the pitfalls of the Ego. Once recognized, it would be transcended as part of the ascension journey into the merging with the Higher Divine-Self. I was happy to say that my Spiritual Ego had now joined the other layers of my ego in my continual progression towards a transcended state.

Self-love

Self-love, therefore, is an act of the transcended Ego and it is not selfishness. Self-love is the result of having achieved the complete understanding of Oneness with the Divine within. The Divine within is the Christ Seed or the God-Spark that we all carry in our heart. Some of us have chosen to hide this Divine part so deep that it's difficult to be able to acknowledge its presence in this lifetime. The blindfold we have put upon ourselves has been truly thick and heavy, blocking Divine Light. The challenge has been to overcome this handicap and discover the presence of Light within and, in so doing, stimulate the thinning of the veil.

Learning to love oneself unconditionally triggers the awareness of the Divine connection within. Therefore, it doesn't make sense to say that you love God when you deny that love to the God-Spark within you. Loving yourself unconditionally is the confirmation of your love of God the Creator. I had reached the opening of this understanding after my healing sessions with Lindsey and had taken my first initiatives in implementing this concept in life.

One woman reached a light-spark moment when she exclaimed: "Oh, I get it now! We are baby God-sparks and for me, it's easy to love babies!"

Loving yourself without any strings attached magnifies the Love energies within the heart and, once filled, it overflows into the ability to love others unconditionally as well. Again, this reminds me of the message flight attendants give to passengers: "Always put the oxygen mask on yourself first." How can you help someone else if you're gasping for breath?

How can you look after your child if you don't look after your own health first? By health I mean all factors of health: physical, emotional, mental and spiritual. An angry, bitter and frustrated parent can have a devastating effect upon a child's development even if the results are not visible immediately.

Being selfish on the other hand is a false kind of love because it has conditions attached to it. For example, a selfish person would buy a gift for a friend with the intent of getting something that she thinks her friend needs. Then she would be hurt if the friend didn't use or show appreciation for the gift. A person who is in Self-Love mode would try to buy something the friend would like to have and be at peace even if the friend did not like the gift.

On many occasions, the women in the circle would ask similar questions regarding low self-esteem challenges. I recalled the discussion we had on this subject and chuckle now at the memory of it. "Do you like beautiful paintings?" I asked one woman in particular who considered herself very unattractive.

"Yes, you know that. You've seen the nice pictures I have on my walls. Why do you ask?"

"If you saw one abstract painting that you did not understand, like a Picasso for instance, or one that you didn't like, would you tell the painter that his work was ugly?"

"Heavens no."

"Why not?"

"He created it; it's his art work. It's good in his eyes. His paintings are worth a lot."

At that point I produced a mirror and asked her to look at herself.

"Why are you doing this? Give the mirror to Mary; she's prettier than I am."

"Who made you?"

"God did, of course!"

"Would you tell him now that his art work that you see in the mirror is ugly and not worth much?"

She thought I was being silly and, although she got the point I was trying to make, she still had a hard time looking at herself as worthy. I understood her dilemma for I had been there before!

Many would ask me: "How do I do this? How do I love myself first?" My response would be: "What have you done for yourself lately? Did you go for that massage? Did you have your hair done? Did you enroll yourself in that course you wanted to take? Did you go see your doctor for your regular checkup? Did you take the time to rest and read that favorite book? Did you allow others to help you when you needed it?"

Where there is a will there is a way, as the saying goes, and excuses just don't work here. No one appreciates a tired, ill and unhappy you. I discovered this the hard way!

Energy Symptoms

Once I was at ease with my ego, I learned to tap more deeply into the energy stream. I discovered that my whole being was affected. I was flooded with a wide range of 'ascension' symptoms that would knock me off my feet for a while.

At first I could only feel the tingling in my hands and feet but it soon spread over my whole body. The most dramatic one was the feeling as if ants were crawling all over my skin and then they started crawling inside my skin. Next came the feeling as if I was plugged into a socket and a vibrator had been turned on inside of me. I later discovered that someone had named this wild tingling, 'spinning.'

My husband continually denies his intuitive side, but this part of him frequently resurfaces during his dream stage. He often talks in his sleep but rarely remembers upon awakening. The increase in my vibration manifested itself in a humorous way on a number of occasions. He was already asleep one night when I went to bed. As soon as I laid down, he suddenly sat up and said:" You are vibrating again, the whole bed is shaking!" His tone of voice was as if he wanted to say: "Stop that!" On another night he again sat up and said: "What's all this blue light doing here? It's everywhere. Who turned on a blue light?" He did not remember a thing the next day!

My friends and I often discussed and compared our odd symptoms, and it would elicit hilarious laughter from all of us. It is important to note here that the symptoms vary from individual to individual. The following list is just a sample of some common ones:

1. Stomach feeling bloated and letting go of a lot of gas

2. Bad breath

3. Repeated sneezing

4. Flu-like symptoms

5. Waking up at 3 or 4 AM

6. Tingling on skin surface

7. Headache especially at the back close to the neck

8. Diarrhea

9. Dizziness

The list can go on and on. Many websites offer a running list of the latest symptoms to look out for. The idea is not to go into panic when it occurs. The physical body is made up of the heaviest, densest energy and it takes time to restructure and recalibrate every cell. Imagine overhauling and cleaning every little piece of an old rusted, dirty engine and then putting it all back together in a new configuration! The next step would be to turn this new engine on and start learning how to use it based on a more sophisticated manual.

This influx of energies is having an effect in every aspect of our lives, whether we want it to or not. The level of consciousness has risen and precipitated a shift that has never happened before in this Universe. The rapid rise in consciousness is very much in line with the fast rise in our technology today. It not only has an effect on technology but it also affects the Earth's weather patterns, and all the energetic bodies, human and otherwise.

My fascination with the new order of things accelerated as I embraced the new concepts channeled through the various angelic sources. My relationship with Spirit reached a new clarity and, at the same time, it gave me a stronger relationship with others and myself. I had always trusted God completely and, with the knowledge of Oneness with the God-Spark within me, I learned to trust my intuitive gifts I had denied for so long. This re-found part of me was definitely put to the test while we searched for our own home.

Chapter Nine

Transplanted Once More

My husband and I both liked the area and decided to begin our search for a new home after living in the cottage for about a year.

As I said earlier, my intuitive messages were getting stronger day by day. After the decision was made to look for a house, I immediately received the following message: "You are to stay at this lake, there is a reason. There is a place waiting for you, look for number nine. Build and we will lead them to you."

Have they been watching Field of Dreams*? I wondered uneasily.*

The Search

I had no idea where this place was and did not share this message with anyone. Part of my husband's job involved traveling around the countryside, which gave him the perfect opportunity to check possible sites for us. He liked the lake area about an hour further north than where we were and insisted that we look at a number of properties there. I agreed but suggested that we keep our options open and also look around the area around the cottage.

And so we drove to many open houses and wooded sites for months. Curiously, not one house or wooded lot met our criteria. My husband must have sensed something for he did find a place in the area he liked and was strangely adamant that we put a bid on it. I was very surprised that he would even consider it, since it was more a summer cottage than a home. It wouldn't accommodate our furniture to begin with, and would require extensive renovation to make it suitable for our needs. I had to evoke my voting rights here! Fortunately my friend Breana, whom we consider as part of the family, was with us and cast her vote in my favor. I knew that patience was required and that 'number nine' would show itself at the right moment in time. I loved these 'coincidences or synchronicities' when they seemed to appear out of nowhere!

The same real estate agent who helped my husband find the cottage was doing some searching for us and, at times, would drive around with us. During one of these excursions, we drove past some beautiful wooded areas. The agent told us not to bother with them because they were out of our price range. "No one has bought any lots there for years, and they are now off the market," he said discouragingly. As we drove by, I noticed that the lots were numbered and towards the end was lot number 9.

Trials and Tribulations

After many unsuccessful exploratory trips I suggested to my husband that we go for a walk on those properties. He enjoyed walking in the woods as much as I did. There was a passable area marked as being lots six, seven and eight. We both loved it. They were estate lots, ranging from four to eight acres each. Homes were already on the first two lots but the rest were beautiful stretches of mature hardwood trees, majestic maples, oak, birch, poplar and basswood, forming an impressive, serene forest.

I knew where I was supposed to be but there were major hurdles to leap over before I could be there. My trust in Spirit was unwavering and, although I sensed some major blockages coming up, I was quite calm about it. There were gentle nudges from my angelic guides to help me throughout this time of trials, such as, "Faith, trust, release the heavy energies of worry and impatience. Enter the stillness of the eye of the storm."

It did not take long for the trials to commence, for our agent called us out-of-the-blue to tell us that those lots were re-listed. My husband told him that we might be interested in looking at lots 7 and 8, since he told us that the owner did not want to sell number 6, which was our first choice. I made no comment, and trusted that Spirit had it all under control so there was no need for me to interfere. In the meantime, we had already accepted an invitation from some friends to join them in Florida for a couple of weeks. We told the agent that we would contact him upon our return.

Imagine our surprise when a very unhappy agent informed us, that lots seven and eight were sold while we were away. He was not pleased with the whole affair, and suggested that we explore lot number three since that was still available.

It was disastrous. We trudged through dense wood, up and down very steep hills and climbed over large rocky formations. It would be very costly and near impossible to develop this property for private habitation. We gave up halfway into the forest and were about to leave the area when the agent suddenly said, "Since you're here anyway, why don't we have a look at number nine. It's just a bit further down the road."

I knew the minute we walked into the five-acre woodlot that I had found my home. There was a sigh of welcome from the huge trees around me, and I felt as if I had entered a sacred chapel. Of course, we both fell in love with it. My husband was excited but puzzled and asked the agent, "Why is this one not sold? It's the best one of the lot." Then he looked at me and sighed in resignation, "You like this one, don't you?"

As the agent had warned us, the price was high but we had nothing to lose and decided to put in a bid anyway. It was a low bid, for that was all we could afford and we were not surprised when it was rejected. The counter bid was still out of our range. That was the first hurdle and the next one to come was even higher.

With frustration and mounting anger, the agent told us that there were specific conditions with the sale of the property that he did not know about. Apparently the municipality in conjunction with the environmental department had put major restrictions on the construction of the septic system in this area. My husband immediately dropped everything when he found out about the restrictive rules. The rules did not make sense and we found it extremely odd.

Everything was at a standstill and we began to look at other options. A house already in existence on the other side of the lake came on the market and we decided to check it out. Although it needed some work to meet our needs, we decided that we liked it enough to put a bid on it. I did not oppose this one, for I kept hearing that soft whisper to be still and so I did.

The same agent was involved in this transaction as well. The poor man was bewildered, and quite agitated when he told us the news. Our offer was rejected completely and there was no counter offer nor was any reason given, yet our bid was close to the asking price. We had no house to sell, and there were no financial restrictions, so it was quite mystifying. (We found out much later that the house was sold at the price we would have presented as a second bid given the chance.)

The saga continued as the landowner of lot nine unexpectedly called us and asked us to meet him at a restaurant. It was an unusual request and our curiosity was piqued. He had another proposal for us. Apparently he had heard through the local grapevine that my husband had made up his mind not to purchase the property. It was uncanny and very peculiar. Since the house deal didn't go through, we decided to make another bid within our affordability range, which was still substantially lower than his asking price. Both my husband and the agent were flabbergasted when the owner accepted the offer, the deal was signed and lot nine was ours!

The Dream Manifested

The third hurdle was the most challenging of all and required all the inner strength I had to go through this test. We still had to face the local government and the building restrictions. Nonetheless I started working on the house plan. I was confident that Spirit would continue to guide me and that the house would be built as planned. We had to wait a year during which we hired a lawyer to help us with this dilemma. We were very much aware of the pollution problems in the lake and had set aside a budget for the construction of a more costly environmentally friendly septic system. We had also planned to build quite a distance away from the lake and wished to keep the land as pristine as possible.

Spring came and there was no response to all our proposals to the building department. We had hired a local contractor and he had already ordered the first batch of building supplies to be delivered in the spring. He and the suppliers were therefore not happy when we could not get the proper building permits. It was a trying time for everyone. The department was notified that we had obtained legal counsel and that we were waiting for their response. The phone call came one morning and, before the day was over, we had been issued all the permits we needed. The house was built that year exactly as we had originally planned it. We moved into our new home on the first snowy day of the year. Instantly, I felt the peace and tranquility. I was home. Another huge miracle had manifested in my life, a home in the forest, upon an ancient land.

We were living in a house whose walls were made with woven bamboo mats in the more affluent part of the slums in Jakarta. The only reason that we could afford to buy this house was because my aunt and uncle could not stand seeing our deplorable living conditions any longer. We had been living in my uncle's storage shed and this house was a luxury for us. There was no glass in the windows, no screens and no curtains either. At least we had one bedroom for three people instead of five. I remember doing my homework in the bedroom, sitting in a chair with my feet on my bed because mice would run across my feet if I had them on the floor. I shudder every time I think of mice!

A tropical night is far from romantic, and could be downright traumatic. Besides the constant buzz of mosquitoes, gecko lizards would crawl all over the ceiling and the walls. I recall screaming with fright when one fell on my face one night. After that, I put something over my head while nervously keeping an eye on the ceiling. To this day, I stay away from any kind of lizard!

Cats were another nuisance. They were one of the animal species that was acceptable as pets in a predominantly Muslim country. Cats were allowed to roam the streets at will and would invade any home, and steal your dinner right off the dinner table in a flash. At night they would hunt for mice and one night, an enthusiastic hunter fell through the mat ceiling as we were eating dinner! I developed an allergic reaction to cats!

~ ~ ~

Many moons ago, I dreamt of a little house in the woods in a far away land where the ground was blanketed with snow. Half a century later, Spirit gifted me with a beautiful brick home with all the luxuries one could think of. Tall stately maples, birch and poplars surround it, their green canopy forming a dome beneath the sky. Besides the numerous bird populations, the playful squirrels and chipmunks provide all the entertainment I want. The occasional visit by deer, moose and Reddy the fox enhance this natural vista. As I gaze out the window of my home, my heart overflows with deep gratitude, wonderment and awe. I prayed for a small house, instead I was granted a large sanctuary.

Chapter Ten

The Third Circle

As soon as I was settled in my new environment, Gloria asked if we could meet again. I had sensed her strong potential when I met her, and was very happy to see her choosing to reconnect with me. Another gifted person, Sheila, joined us and thus the third Meditation Lightcircle was formed one cold January morning. We met once a week and, for the first few months, it was just the three of us. It was a very relaxed, joyful coming together of like-minded sisters. We diligently worked on ourselves, supporting each other and moving deeper into spiritual awareness. We shared our tears but also a lot of laughter and a lot of snacks! I enjoyed cooking and loved to experiment with new dishes, which meant, of course, that I needed people to test them on. I had found willing candidates! It became a running joke that: "You never know what you are eating when you visit Jinna!"

Field of Dreams

Astonishingly the message: "Build and we will guide them to you," was not long in coming true. Just by word of mouth, more spiritual seekers came to join us. Some stayed and some left, never to return. There was disappointment, of course, but I explained that it was all in perfect order. Everyone had free will and thus free choice according to what they wanted to learn in their lifetime. Each had his/her own path to travel and his/her own lesson plan to follow. Our challenge was to stay centered within the heart, release our attachment to wanting to help everyone and release him or her with love and compassion.

A core group eventually settled into a steady circle with both Gloria and Sheila still attending the meetings whenever they could.

Each participant brought a wealth of knowledge to the circle and I thoroughly enjoyed learning from each one. I had emphasized from the start that we were all students and teachers together and I had as much to learn from them as they from me.

We continued to examine the heavier energies we all carried, and were determined to release as much as possible with each other's support. The trauma of war and violence plus layers of abuse and abandonment issues of the past were the most painful sections for many of us including myself.

"I don't understand this child," my mother's frustrated voice resurfaced within me. "I have never heard of any five-year-old continually trying to run away from home. No matter how hard I spank her, she keeps doing it! What have I ever done to deserve a child like this?"

My parents had left the island where I was born to search for better living conditions, since employment opportunities for young men were almost non-existent. My mother decided to take the youngest child, my eight-month-old sister, and the quiet, four-year-old, leaving me, the two-year-old, with my grandmother.

I was reunited with my parents at the age of five and rebelled for months against living with these strangers who called themselves my mother and father. It was a traumatic period for the whole family and my parents could not comprehend why a child that young suddenly developed severe digestive problems, which added to their exasperation with my behavior.

It took me years to face these layers of abandonment and rejection, and reach the acceptance and understanding of the lesson.

With the permission of the group, I would like to share some of their great stories, beginning with a wonderful couple who chose to join us. We were all very happy to welcome the first male, brave enough to link with a predominantly female gathering. Helmut and Trudy were a delightful pair, enthusiastically entering every session, workshop or class I organized during the next few years.

I was puzzled at Trudy's energy when I first met her. It was very different, something I had not encountered before and I was intrigued. She was a very loving, shy woman who had difficulty joining in our conversations. She had a hearing problem and since her birth speech was German, English did not always give her the clarity she wanted. She felt comfortable with me because I spoke German and knew that she could always ask for a translation afterwards in private. The energy she carried was a very powerful ancient stream but she had not been awakened to it yet. As soon as I began to question her in regards to her ancestry, I became very excited. She was born in Romania and had to face the ugliness of war-torn Europe. She was a direct descendant from the ancient Romanian gypsy tribes! I had read many stories about the strong psychic abilities that the gypsy women had, and thought it fantastic to be able to connect with such a different energy pattern. She was steadfast in her determination to heal herself and, with compassion and love, we held the safe healing space for this reawakened lightworker.

Helmut was our forestry expert and we had great excursions into the forest. Under his supervision, we hunted for wild mushrooms, wild berries and healing herbs for teas and tinctures. He taught me how to tap the sugar maples and I soon had my own supply of maple syrup, while he had his supply of maple sap wine! We sang to the trees, we honored them with sacred tobacco, asked permission to tap them in the spring and then we thanked the generous maple grove. The end result was bottles of high-energy maple syrup. When I gifted a number of bottles to my friends, they could not believe the vibration it held. I gave a local chef a taste of my homemade syrup and he was surprised at the quality. He said that it was exceptionally good and asked me what my secret was. I refrained from telling him that I sing and talk to my trees.

The next couple who joined us was another great addition to the circle. Violet had been on the spiritual path for many years on her own and told me how sad she was that her husband could not share her journey. Randy, her husband, had not shown any interest at all until he came to me for a massage. We talked and shared information as we got to know each other during these sessions. He became interested in the sweat lodge ceremonies and asked if he could join me.

It was an instant awakening for him that night. He was seated across from me in the lodge and told us later how shocked he'd been when he saw my eyes glowing before him. He also saw the animal spirits enter and the manifestation of Light beams during the ceremony. His sensitivity was aroused and from that moment on, he was able to sense the energy flow. He could 'feel' me standing behind him and often times would ask me to move when my field was a bit too strong for him that day. He did not question his wife any longer after this experience and both came to our gatherings whenever they could. It was a moving moment for me to see them both attending and enjoying the meditation and healing circle.

Human Angelic Guides

The enhanced intuitive ability allowed me to sense the strong potential strands emanating from certain people and I would try to encourage them to develop this gift. With the Harmonic Convergence, the call went out for potential Master Teachers to awaken but not many answered. I had been made aware that that was what I was being groomed for – to teach and prepare the Master Teachers who will be in great demand as the Great Shift progresses. The lessons were not easy; hard work and unwavering commitment were the prerequisite for this Master's class. Of those who did answer the call, not many were able to withstand the rigors and the fast pace of the New Energy Path and thus some left to find a more suitable path. One of the greatest challenges was, of course, the awareness of the Spiritual Ego and reaching the level of ego transcendence. Spiritual competition was another heavy energy and, unfortunately, a very strong temptation for many Lightworkers. I had been vigilant and intent to continue to be mindful to avoid these spiritual pitfalls and thank my guides profusely for assisting me in this area.

The core group that persevered and continued to walk with me were ones I coined Human Angelic Guides. Missy was one such hidden light-beam. Missy and I had been friends for a very long time and would reconnect off and on through the years. I began to send her a message when I sensed her potential awakening gaining in strength. It was the same message over and over again: "Are you ready?" She had no idea, of course, what it was all about and tried to ignore me by saying, "No." It became a humorous game that we played for a while until her curiosity propelled her into my space.

These Human Angelic Guides are truly the wave of new Masters who teach by the way they live and how they walk the path. I am deeply honored to be of service to all these magnificent Lighthouses and would like to thank each one for choosing to walk with me for a section of my journey.

New Energy Reiki

Our focus was also to continue to work on healing and clearing all the blockages in our own energetic fields. We met once a week, meditating in the morning and practicing energy healing in the afternoon. We continued to use the term 'meditation' although it had evolved into deeper inner work and I would often refer to it as Energy Centering. The afternoon sessions worked well, but sometimes there was not enough time for deeper individual work, especially when a major block was detected. I would set aside another day in this case to facilitate a one-on-one healing session, or a two-on-one with another member of the group assisting.

The effect on the healing energies were at first very subtle until I noticed changes in the Reiki energy. Since becoming a Reiki Master, I had facilitated many healing sessions and as I tapped into the higher frequencies of the New Energies, my Reiki sessions were shifting and flowing into a whole new level of healing work. Some of the women began to feel the difference when I worked on them and asked me to teach this new version. Thus the New Energy Reiki became an innovative level of healing modality for all of us. It was still Reiki; however, we learned how to 'plug into the higher voltage' and found the results to be amazing.

I recalled how I wanted to heal everyone when I first learned Reiki. I would offer it to anyone and try to persuade him or her to try it again despite their reluctance to do so. With the new energy, this temptation became even more pronounced.

I learned very quickly that no one can heal another person; we can only hold the healing space. They have to be accountable for their own healing. I cannot take responsibility for another person's healing, for it's not my body. The body knows what's best for its own healing, and all it needs is someone to help hold an energetic safe space so the healing can occur. A doctor can operate and help you begin your healing process, but you are ultimately responsible for taking your medicines and taking the rest needed to heal yourself.

Healing will always happen when a person asks for a healing session, but it will often not be visible in the physical if the subconscious decides that it still needs the lessons of the illness. The healing will occur at the etheric levels and slowly permeate down into the physical when the person is ready to accept his/her life lesson. Energy healing is not a pill that you can take and expect an instant cure. It works on many levels of your being because you are made up of many layers – spiritual, emotional, mental and physical. Healing is a holistic process and each layer requires a healing before the whole unit can be whole again. The most difficult areas of imbalance to acknowledge are the ones that cannot be perceived with the human eye and are, therefore, often ignored or discarded.

Relationships

The layer of relationships is one such area and a very complicated one to face, let alone heal. It is a huge subject area and requires an in-depth study. My intent is only to discuss a small part that is relevant to my story in order to bring greater understanding of the relationships within a group dynamic.

As more and more people came to explore our meetings, it was inevitable that some friction would occur between participants. It was therefore not a surprise when I was asked to ban or deny admittance to certain individuals. This disturbed me and filled me with deep sadness. Compassion flooded my heart as I refused such a request. I realized that those making the demand did not yet understand the lessons I had brought forth. It was painfully difficult but I knew that I had to take a step back, detach and release my connection to allow the choice of Free Will. I love them all and it was not easy to let them go, however I had absolute faith that these angels-in-training will continue with their learning in different ways. Each choice is honored, for I repeat, there are no wrong or right ones in the Eyes of the Creator.

The higher the frequency of energy, the more you begin to merge with the Oneness of All Things. In this state of Be-ing, there are no boundaries between each person, although each will retain their own uniqueness within. Thus for me, existing in the higher vibration means that I accept everyone in my space without fear, no matter at what level of vibration that person may be. If there still is resentment on my part towards a person, it will be a big mirror for me to look at. It is essential then for me to re-examine my own darkness, my own issues that I have not forgiven myself for and which I have not released.

A Being who vibrates at a higher frequency is like a strong beam of light. No darkness can exist in a bright light of Love energy. A very bright flashlight easily penetrates the darkness and nothing can stain or mar a shining light. Darkness cannot exist nor attach itself to Light.

A person who is still choosing to play in the darkness is like a dark room. When that person enters my space, I am honored for I know that she or he has chosen me to be the lamp to illuminate the dark corners. A room full of light does not need another lamp but a shadowy room that only has a dim light in it does. There is nothing for me to be afraid of or anything for me to do except to stand still and hold my light as bright as I can to help the person 'see' the areas that were hidden before. The same idea can be applied to a place of employment. It is another area of opportunity to shine your light, for your co-workers are often your biggest mirrors of your karmic records.

I have always considered Jesus to be one such bright 'lamp.' I recall the Bible stories narrating his life, and how he would enter the homes of people who were shunned by others. He associated himself with the lowest members of society, those considered 'sinners.' I do not think that his Light was ever affected nor dimmed for He is in Oneness with the Father Creator, the highest frequency, The Source of Love and Light itself.

Chapter Eleven

The Divine Feminine Energy

Besides the revival of the Light Circle group, I sensed that a new chapter of my life was about to unfold in this new home. My spiritual quest was on hold while the house was being built and I was now anxious to continue. I felt that there was so much more for me to learn and I could hardly wait to experience each new manifestation of energy in my field.

I dove back into my studies, both in the healing arts as well as metaphysical subjects. I intended to broaden my horizon and to magnify my scope of understanding at the fastest pace possible. To gain a more thorough knowledge, I took a deeper look at the earth's energetic history.

Rebalancing

For eons, the Male Energies had dominated the Earth and this created an imbalance in frequencies. It reminded me of two musical notes that were not in tune and thus there was no harmony of sound. With the arrival of the Harmonic Convergence came an opportunity to bring balance into the Universe. To eliminate the discrepancy caused by the dominant male component, there had to be a substantial influx of Divine Feminine Love Energies.

The Harmonic Convergence was the permit that initiated the big shift towards balance. The Divine Feminine Energies are now unstoppable, radiating, entering through major star gates, and flooding every aspect of our being. This strong feminine love energy is causing many levels of fear, especially within the Male Energy. We all have both male and female attributes within us and for millennia we existed in an imbalanced state, with the male side taking the lead role. For those who have a dominant male side, this situation can be very threatening, especially if looked upon as a struggle for power, a win or lose war zone. The male ego has difficulty with the lovey-touchy-feely female way of expression. This unrestricted outpouring of affection is just not 'macho' to many males and it is to be avoided at all cost!

"Take that doll away from that child, he's a boy! Stop hugging and kissing him, he's a boy. Tell him to stop crying, men don't cry!" My aunt's disgusted voice jarred across the room as she watched her daughter playing with her son. Even the women were buying into this male-macho make-up and seemed to desire it as well. Many times had I overheard the women discussing husband potentials. "You can't let her marry him. Look at him. He is weak like a woman. He even walks like a woman. I saw him cry! What a sissy!"

The dominant male does not understand that there is no struggle for domination on the female side. There are no losers or winners. The Female Energy is only rising to bring in the balance with unconditional love and compassion. It is like a scale, where the female side has been weighted down by control, disrespect, and abuse. Now I see this scale slowly rising to meet the Male part, to stand beside him in equal partnership and create the peace and harmony we all yearn for. It is to the benefit of all to achieve balance and become One in Spirit.

The Magnetic Grid

The Earth's magnetic grid had to be recalibrated, restructured to allow the increased flow of the Love energy. I saw it as changing the wiring of an old house with only a 100-volt capacity to one that would handle 1000 volts. I was sure that keeping the old wiring would burn any house down given this scenario.

To my amazement, I was gifted with an invitation by the angelic hosts to witness the completion of the new magnetic grid that was restructured by the Kryon entourage. Kryon, the angelic entity, came with his entourage after the Harmonic Convergence with the specific purpose of changing the 'wiring' of the earth's magnetic field. Someone began to call it the Kryon grid and it took a number of years to complete.

It was December 31st, 2002 and I felt odd that day, out of sorts, not quite understanding the why of it. My youngest daughter was home and for some reason I asked her to turn off all the electronic equipment in the room, including her CD player. Being an Indigo child, she only looked at me and proceeded to fulfill my request without any questions.

It was a tradition that we would play a card game after dinner and then have a special Dutch treat called 'olie bollen' at midnight when we welcomed the New Year. I had made this treat for years and all it required was to prepare the dough to rise so that it was ready by eleven to be cooked. I tried twice and both batches did not turn out that well. It did not seem to bother me for I kept feeling increasingly disconnected as the evening progressed. We began playing our card game and I kept laughing, thinking everything to be hilarious, especially when I didn't seem to care or know what cards I had. Nobody relished me as a partner that night!

I felt part of me floating in the void somewhere and heard the invitation to move upwards, while another part of me tried to play the card game. There in a huge circle around the Earth were thousands of Lightbeings. One reached his hand to me and invited me to sit beside him, as if we were part of an audience in a theatre. I felt extremely privileged and could sense the excitement as we watched an extraordinary golden web-like grid closing around the Earth. "Look," my companion said, as he pointed to the center of the grid. "Kryon did promise to put a bow on it when it is completed."

The sound of musical cheers erupted to celebrate the completion of this tremendous undertaking. Shimmering waves of Love, joy and exuberance rippled across this remarkable gathering.

A friend of mine intended to call me that day to wish me a Happy New Year and her guides had advised her to phone me earlier if she wished to speak to me because they told her that I would be gone later that evening. She got busy and forgot to keep an eye on the time. When she finally phoned me after dinner, she said that my voice was very different and she realized that she was too late because a big part of me had already left.

The magnetic grid was just one of the major changes to accommodate the arrival of the Divine Feminine Energy and many more other 'wirings' would be changed for the next several years.

It was no coincidence that many of the angelic helpers of the feminine vibration were now making themselves more available to us. Quan Yin of course was one of them and her presence was opening the gates for the increase of the energies of Compassion and Divine Love.

Guide Energy

More guide energy is now available to us and I decided to take advantage of this wonderful source of guidance. For example, Archangel Michael's monthly transmissions channeled through Ronna Herman were another welcome addition to my source of information. I received a couple of short readings from this wondrous entity and it confirmed my strong affinity with him.

I was thrilled with his validation of my connection with St.Germain and the Violet Flame. He also emphasized my strong connection with the Earth Mother and my past history as a healer.

I had frequently sensed Michael's presence but, being human, I often wondered why he would come to me. This reservation was one day blown out of the water during a massage treatment. The therapist was an intuitive healer and she shared the following with me as I relaxed on her table.

"This has never happened during any other massages I have ever given, but a huge angelic entity has just come in. There is so much light, it fills this whole room. This is so extraordinary, and I'm not sure what to make of it. I feel as if I am in a powerful loving presence. A male energy presence."

I asked her to request his name. His answer had us both in tears. "It is Archangel Michael. He says he has come because you have been asking for validation. Have you been working with Archangel Michael?" I have not doubted his presence ever since.

Since that incident, I tried to pay more attention to all the information I encountered as I continued my journey. I diligently examined every article and message from a variety of metaphysical sources and discerned the ones that spoke to my heart. It made me reflect on the implications of this shift for all creation, as we know it. It was exciting yet at the same time it filled me with apprehension, a familiar sensation indeed.

~ ~ ~

I was standing on the deck of a luxurious cruise liner watching the shores of my birth country slowly disappear. Besides having lived in Singapore, which was just next-door so to speak, I had never journeyed this far across the ocean. I was filled with anticipation but also with trepidation. My mind was filled with apprehension as I wondered, *What will I encounter when I reach this strange new land so far across the Indian Ocean? Will the people there accept me? Will I be able to earn enough to make a decent living? How will I survive these changes?*

My parents told us that they could only provide a one-way ticket for each of us, so there was no going back. This was truly a one-way trip, for deep in my heart I knew that it would be very unlikely that I would ever see this country again. I watched with melancholy as this tropical paradise faded from my sight. I regretfully pondered the fact that this wondrous land could harbor such devastating horror and sadness. My life as I knew it had ended and I had to face a new unknown future with trust and faith in God as my only guide.

I was on my way to Germany, the 'white-man's country' as we called it. I had read all the stories but was I prepared to meet and interact with this new culture and belief system? I had studied the language and was proficient enough to survive. Germany was the only country that was willing to issue work visas for Indonesian citizens at that time. It was our only choice, for we had no money and had to work for a living. We each received a two-year visa and after that the future was again a huge question mark. I was young enough that I did not dwell too much on that uncertain prospect.

What I encountered was a small piece of a fairy tale I was so fond of reading. The German people I met were the friend-liest and most accommodating group I could ever dream about. They took me into their homes and their hearts as if I was part of the family. A couple of ladies even tried their best to convince me to become their daughter-in-law. I declined gracefully and regretfully. I enjoyed my life and appreciated all the new exciting things I learned and experienced but somehow I never felt at home there.

I began to comprehend the intricacies of constantly having to recalibrate and adapt to the changes of frequencies in the energy field. The great shift for me felt just like the voyage when I had sailed across unfamiliar ocean waters to a strange New World. In a sense, I was asking the same anxious questions, "What will this new Earth be for us? How will we survive all the changes? Will the angelic guides help us maneuver these uncharted waters?"

The key here was to release all FEAR-based reactions, for fear is just an absence of knowledge. Imagine the terror of an aborigine in the Amazon jungles a few decades ago when encountering an airplane for the first time! Their fear dissolved once they gained information about aerodynamics and enjoyed a plane ride.

'The Shift of the Ages' is nothing more than just a shift in human consciousness. It is a shift in the belief systems that make up our personal realities. It is a definite shift in awareness, the same way that I shifted my perception and my belief systems when I entered a whole new way of life. For all of us, the old way of life will slowly fade from our view just like the scene I went through.

The wheels of change have been set in motion and their rotation is increasing in speed. Nothing here on Earth can stop this momentum. There are no emergency brakes to pull. The only thing that we can influence is our willingness to change our belief systems and our attitudes as we begin to embrace a new way of life based on love not war.

Changing of the Guards

Based upon this understanding, a number of things had to happen to facilitate the Shift. Everything, including all the energies of the angelic helpers who had stayed within the Earth plane, needed to be repositioned as well. Many lightworkers who were well along on their path of awakening found that their personal guides had one day left the neighborhood. It caused an absolute panic until they understood that the guides did not really leave in the way humans think!

We were all born with a set of guardian angels and guides, who held our hands and protected us like a loving mother would. As we chose to move into enlightenment, we entered a new level of awareness and development. In other words, with the influx of new energy, we outgrew the sandbox and were now ready to graduate to grade one. As a mother, I knew how it felt when I had to leave my child at the classroom door for the first time. Although tears were clouding my eyes, I gently pried my daughter's desperate hands from mine and left her with the new teacher. I would never leave my child but I could lovingly watch as she bravely entered the halls of higher learning. In the same manner, the guides lovingly released our hands. They distanced themselves, observing with love, ready to come to our assistance whenever we ask.

There were moments of panic and grief when they let go of me. I felt the similar anxious feeling in my gut when I first had to ride my bike without anyone holding it. The same fearful panic I could see in a toddler's eyes when mom let go, for the child's first walk alone.

I had taken my tentative, halting steps into the higher vibration and was just beginning to learn all the new ropes. What had confused so many others and myself was the fact that the changes were coming so fast. It reminded me of the frustration my husband had when his office continually changed the computer programs. He had just been trained on one system and before he could really get into it, it was changed into a whole new system again.

Albert Einstein once said, *"Change is the only constant in the Universe."* He was right but this time the rate of shift changes was in direct correlation to the changes in human consciousness. Since we had all agreed at Spirit level to move ahead, it gave the acceleration the green light. New guides were entering, surfing in through the gamma rays that the Sun had been emitting to the puzzlement of the scientific community. There were reports of very unusual high amounts of gamma rays that burst forth at unprecedented levels of intensity.

Master Guides

Through the channeled messages, we began to understand that these were the Energies of the Master Guides coming in for those who were moving into the higher vibrational levels.

Being an ex-teacher, I think of it as entering higher educational classrooms and studying with the Master Teachers. You cannot stay with your Kindergarten teacher when you have decided to fast track and enter high school. Many of us have chosen to step up, to increase the speed of our development, and thus new Master Guides are needed to help us in this process. It is just the changing of the Guards.

The changes were increasing at an unprecedented pace and the overall process continued to accelerate. The time came when another level of Master Guides, which included the avatars, the goddesses, and the Ascended Masters who had stayed in the Earth plane to help us, left as well. Their energies needed to be readjusted, too. It was just a different kind of changing of the guards.

All those who were highly sensitive to the energy stream felt the disconnection, the emptiness and sadly waited for their return.

All the old energies of the lower dimension had to be released to make room for the new order of things. It would be the same as renovating a room. You had to tear down and throw out all the old parts first before you could begin building the new parts.

I did not know what to expect and hoped for their speedy return. We needed all the help we could get to help us through this tremendous recalibration process of ascension. When they did return, their energetic make-up was different, for they were fully in tune with the higher frequencies. The most important message for me was that Quan Yin had taken on the mantle of the Divine Feminine Gateway and was now prepared to hold this gate for as long as it takes to help us move through the changes.

Chapter Twelve

The Lotus Blossom

The Loving compassionate energies of Quan Yin had been with me ever since Lindsey reintroduced her to me. I understood then that she was part of the embodiment of the Divine Feminine Energy now flowing into the Earth's energetic matrix, and I was thrilled to get to know her better. I offered her my help and again, in my innocence, did not quite know what I was volunteering for. I started feeling her presence at the cottage and could sometimes feel her loving gentle touch on my cheek or on my hair. I loved her gentle energy and basked in her loving embrace.

State of Infancy

My dreams and visions continued to paint my sleep patterns and often bubbled up during a deep meditation or lucid dream state.

The following is a narration of a number of visions that threw me into a turbulent flow of change upon change in my life. The impact of these signs exposed new directions for me and it took a lot of courage for me to put my feet upon these pathways.

The first notable vision was brought to me in a dream state after we had moved into the new house. I was walking with Quan Yin and she escorted me to the end of a semi-circular marble patio. There were steps going right down into a lagoon or bay. "Look," she said as she softly nudged me closer to the water. As I looked into the water, a lotus stem emerged out of the water and green leaves sprouted from it. The next scenes were similar to an action photography sequence that would capture a flower in the process of blooming. A lotus bud grew in between the floating leaves and kept growing into a beautiful large pink and white blossom. As the petals began to unfurl, I noticed a strange, watery object moving inside the flower. It was a water-baby! It was a live baby but its whole body was made out of water. I could see right through him! It startled me when suddenly the baby was in my arms. It was really cute. It gurgled and moved its arms and legs just like any other baby; it was soft and fluid like water but contained in a crystal baby form.

I did not know what to think about it when I woke up. I knew it was a vision because I could remember it vividly upon awakening. Normally, if it was a dream, I could only keep it in my memory for so long unless I wrote it down immediately.

I understood part of it because I was aware that the Crystal Energies were part of the new energy flow. The child then must be a representation of the new crystal children that were about to enter the Earth. This deduction somehow didn't feel right, so I asked if any of my psychic friends could help me gain more clarity. The only response was that it was all about me and the answer was within me. When I went within and asked the Goddess for clarity, there was only silence.

Life Lessons

To my consternation I was beginning to feel a deep blockage that was coming to the surface. I was in need of another healing session myself. I hadn't figured out what the baby vision was all about and deduced that this was perhaps beginning to get to me. I asked Sheila to guide me into a private healing session. She agreed to accommodate me one day and I put myself into a deep healing trance state.

I was shocked at what I encountered. I thought I'd already released all the major issues with Lindsey but here they were, back in my face ... or shall I say, in my body. The pain and the anguish were not as severe but nonetheless, they still pounded my body as I gave it permission to release whatever residue there was. Sheila joined me in tears as she told me that she saw Quan Yin holding me and saw many other Lightbeings crowding in the room holding the healing space. I was grateful and thanked all of them but was nonetheless perturbed. "What's going on?" I asked. "Why did all this compacted energy re-enter to be released again?" I needed some answers.

Enter the Group and Steve Rother. The Group is a group of angelic entities that channel their messages through Steve Rother. I attended a number of seminars given by Steve and his wife, Barbara, in Toronto and immediately felt a rapport with them. I persuaded Steve to present the Group in a seminar here in the North and a wonderful friendship was established between us. To this day, both of them continue to play a major role in my on-going spiritual process. Their love and compassion for me has sustained me through some painful periods in my life. I will always cherish their friendship and consider them part of my Spiritual family.

I attended the Spiritual Psychology course with Steve and Barbara and it opened a whole vista of deeper understanding.

It helped me to understand what my life lessons were, what I had scripted and planned for this present incarnation.

Just like choosing your major and your minor subjects in college, so too do we choose our life lessons for our human incarnations. We all have to deal with all twelve life lessons the same way a student has to study all subjects of the core curriculum. But we can choose a major subject and sometimes two, called an Energy Matrix. We come in 'wired' for this Matrix and it will stay with us for the duration of this lifetime. It cannot be healed but it can be mastered. According to Steve, "Mastery is finding positive uses for negative attributes." [1]

In other words, Mastery does not mean that it's gone; it only means that you are now aware of it and accept it as part of your make-up. Once that is established, you can find new and creative ways of using it to achieve the highest outcome for yourself. "Once mastered, a matrix never needs to be repeated as the mastery becomes part of your core personality and thus remains with you from one lifetime to the next." [2]

The minor lesson is called an Energy Stamp, and these can be healed within one lifetime. "Energy Stamps are a particular form of energy that gets imprinted on us through certain experiences during a particular lifetime."[3]

We choose these stamps to help us with our lessons and it can be perceived as negative or positive. The Stamps once imprinted are carried on an energy tube that runs from the top of your head down the spinal column, through the root into the ground.[4] The tube is the seat of the emotions and any energy fluctuations in the tube will result in strong emotional turbulence. Emotional pain results when the creative light energy hits these

[1] *Spiritual Psychology* pg 99
[2] *Spiritual Psychology* pg 100
[3] *Spiritual Psychology* pg 102
[4] *Spiritual Psychology* pg 83

blockages in the tube and if not healed will manifest as physical illness. The blockages can be released through intense energy healing sessions similar to the ones I went through with Lindsey. I finally understood what happened to me during those first healing sessions. Once released, the indentation of the stamp is not completely removed. There is a residue, like scar tissue, that still remains on the tube. As the tube expands and stretches due to increased input of higher energy levels, the scar tissue is stretched as well and will cause a rebound effect. Residue of old issues will resurface and another release is activated but at a much reduced level of intensity.

My intense work on myself had precipitated my energy tube's expansion and now I was dealing with all the scar tissue. It was the core of the onion! I realized then, I still had emotional attachments to many of my former heavy issues. It prompted me to seek closure, to completely eliminate as many scar tissues as I could. I began to write letter after letter, asking forgiveness and forgiving each one with compassion and Love. I addressed my parents, my family and any other person in my life who came to hold the mirror for me to see who I am. I found out that you are never finished with tears as I sobbed my way through page after page. Finally I gathered them all and built a sacred fire. Then I asked the wind to carry the ashes into the compassionate heart of the Universe.

Once more, I lay on the healing table, wanting to make sure that I had completely eradicated the major scar tissues. I could hear Sheila beginning to tone; she has a beautiful voice and it carried me deeper within. I felt a gentle touch and saw Quan Yin bending over me placing a beautiful lotus blossom in my heart. It took root there and began to grow, completely cradling me within its beautiful pink petals that were edged in gold and silver. I could feel my arms mimicking the unfolding of the lotus petals and they were in that position when I came back to awareness. Tears of joy cascaded from my eyes as our voices joined in thanksgiving. I could not thank my friend enough for facilitating the healing session for me.

The second vision burst into my dream state soon after. I was back at the same patio with Quan Yin behind me. I sensed her smiling at me as she pointed at the water's surface. Just like the first one, the lotus emerged out of the water and began to bloom. I happily anticipated seeing the cute baby again and was not prepared for what I saw. It was not a baby any longer; the water being who flowed out of the lotus was the most exquisite naked female body I have ever admired. She was made out of rippling, flowing water and she rose out of the lotus, arms outstretched to the sky greeting the morning sun. Her head was tilted back as she lifted her face to the heavens while her long watery hair rippled and shimmered in the golden rays of the sun.

At last I understood the vision of the water baby. It was a gift of the lotus to show me that we are graduating from the infant state into a mature adult female figure that represented the Divine Feminine Energy within all of us. It also made me aware of the important aspect of water and I resolved to study it further.

Waterways

The answer to my enquiry came swiftly through a website that somehow was brought to my attention. It was the site of Water-Consciousness. I e-mailed Dr.Corridor in Australia and she told me that Undine, a water entity had come to awaken another part of me into awareness. As I read her message, it struck a deep cord within me, and I knew that I had to walk this path, as well.

I had always had a love/hate relationship with water. I love the lakes and the oceans of the Earth but at the same time I am terrified of the possibility of drowning. Water scenes have a peaceful tranquil effect on me as long as I have my feet firmly planted upon the earth. My love affair with water was one of the reasons I insisted that we built on a waterfront property.

Dr. Emoto's work with the crystalline structure of water was another fascinating phenomenon that came to my attention. The results of his water experiments were astounding. I encourage everyone to read his reports and his books on the effects of the energy of Love on water molecules. After all, we are beings primarily made up of mostly water, so it was exciting to know that we can influence the structure of our water content with Love energy.

Dr. Corridor on the other hand works with the Water Beings – whales, dolphins and the water entities. She informed me that one of her assignments was to reawaken the ancient Water Priestesses. It was time for this ancient awareness to come forth and help Gaia, the Earth Mother, to clear her etheric waterways in preparation of the massive changes to come.

Gaia is a sentient being and her waterways are similar to our circulatory system. Unfortunately, the pollution that we have produced for many years has taken its toll and this area also needs to be cleared.

All illnesses and imbalances begin in our energetic bodies and, when not healed, descend and manifest in the physical. When we create a blockage or imbalance in our emotional, mental and spiritual bodies, it begins to act like a wound and unless healed will show in our physical bodies as an illness. It is just like an untreated cut that gets infected. The combined blockages of humanity have affected Gaia's energetic and physical bodies as well. We are part of the Earth and she is part of us. The phrase: "from ashes to ashes and from dust to dust" reminds us of this association at every funeral.

As I understood it, the role of a Water Priestess was to help clear the blockages in both the physical and etheric layers. This can be done through connecting the Earth's waterways to generate a current of energy. To my amazement, she told me that I was a Water Priestess and that it was now time for me to awaken to that talent to help clear the waterways of Mother Earth. She asked me to meet her and join one of her seminars but it was not possible for me to do so at that time.

I was on my own and at first was not quite sure how and where to begin. I was aware that the knowledge was dormant within my memory, and it only needed a key to unlock this ancient file. I am continually amazed at how Spirit quietly arranges for the key to appear and for things to happen!

The Arctic Current

My husband was discussing our holiday plans when he announced that he would really like to venture to the North that summer. "How far north?" I asked.

"All the way to James Bay. We live in a very interesting part of the country. About four hours north of our lake there's an underground natural division. This divide causes the water flow to split, one to flow north into James Bay that connects to the Arctic Ocean and one to flow south where the water eventually will flow into the Atlantic Ocean. Amazingly we're living on top of the Southern Flow."

Our friend Breana was going to join us and before I knew it, we were driving north. I had received the intuitive guidance to make special preparations for the journey and so I carried a small bottle of our lake water in my purse.

We stopped at the small marker on the side of the road that indicated the divide where the two flows went their separate ways. As I stood beside the marker for my husband to take a picture to remind us of the moment, I reflected on how that marker had a deeper meaning for me, for I was very conscious of the etheric flow that was superimposed over the physical one.

We came to the end of the highway in the town of Cochrane. There were no more major roads heading north from this point on, so the next morning, we boarded the Polar Bear Express train for another five hours to the town of Moosonee. We stayed there for three days and had an interesting and very educational visit.

On the second day, we joined a group of tourists on a small boat for an excursion into James Bay. I felt the energy shifting as I entered the boat and knew that the Water Beings would inform me when the time was right. I heard the captain's announcement the minute we entered the Bay.

I went to the aft deck, where a lot of people milled around but oddly, I was suddenly alone. I took advantage of this private moment and poured the lake water into the murky rolling waters beside the boat. I invited the Water Spirits to help connect the waterways of the Earth as the liquids merged. At that very instant, I was overwhelmed by a very strong emotion of deep heart-wrenching sadness and sense of loss. Tears streamed down my cheeks as I sobbed my heart out. It was as if all of the elements were grieving and saying goodbye to the old familiar way of things. I found myself chanting a song of mourning, but couldn't remember what it was afterwards. Then I heard a soft sigh, a soft breeze and it was done. A final chant, a final whisper in the wind, "It is done, it is done, it is done, and so be it." It was an extraordinary moment. I felt empty but not sad any more, my tears disappeared, and I was left in a melancholic state.

Suddenly a lot of people began wandering the deck all around me again. Breana knew what I had planned and she was a bit concerned when she saw me: "Are you all right?"

"I'm fine. It has begun." I smiled.

I shared this story with the group when I came back and strangely, I was not surprised when Gloria with moist eyes put something in my hand. She herself had just returned from her trip out West. She said that she heard the message for her to pick up the stone at her feet and bring it to me. At that moment, she was standing on an icy glacier somewhere in the mountains. We gently placed the stone that carried the vibration of ancient frozen water into our lake connecting the west to the east.

My journey did not stop there, for at different times of that year, I found myself traveling, criss-crossing the North American continent, finally ending up in the west in Hawaii. Wherever I went, I was mindful of the waterways, and felt as if I was pulling a golden thread connecting the etheric flow like a spider's web.

I discovered that I was also a Crystal Elder, a very old Soul who had now come full circle. I had received many messages and readings from different channels throughout my journey and accepted each gift gratefully. I understood that ultimately the answers I seek were already within me. The messages were all different because they flowed through each unique individual and therefore carried the person's flavor.

Diversity is the intent of the Universe and has always been. We would all be fed up and bored out of our minds if we had only one flavor or one kind of anything to choose from. I take what resonates within my heart and follow my own guidance accordingly, with full awareness of the possibility of a sidestep of the Spiritual Ego from its path of transcendence.

It made sense now why I was receiving numerous crystal gifts, many of them crystal lotuses. The gifts were given to me in both the physical and in the dimensional realms. Crystal roses and crystal medallions were also part of the surprises for me.

Chapter Thirteen

The Goddesses

I understand why some people have difficulty with the name 'Goddess,' because it has the flavor of ancient deity worship. According to the dictionary, 'Goddess' means 'Female God.' Male and female attributes are created for the human existence of duality, for God has no gender the way humans do. Therefore, for me, it is again just a human word to describe a Divine Feminine energy that many ancient belief systems are already familiar with. We in the West are only just beginning to recognize the significance of this Unconditional Love energy, channeled through the Divine Feminine vessels called 'Goddesses.' I look at it as a term of endearment, a name of honor to the vessels that carry this Creative, Love, God energy.

Quan Yin

I had accepted the fact that somehow this gentle Goddess of Compassion and Love had chosen me to be part of her entourage. Frequently, I would receive messages from other channels as I had mentioned before and it further validated what I had already noticed. Nonetheless, it still filled me with wonder that I was part of this amazing energy.

The intensity of the Quan Yin energy rose in accordance with the influx of the new energy waves, and I could sense the strength of the meld when it happened. I was in constant communication with her now and her aspect seemed to be fully integrated within my consciousness. Curiously, this melding of aspects was visible at times to some people. Dora, another member of our group, was startled when I came through the door one morning. She had a very strange look on her face. "Are you all right?" I asked.

"I'm fine," she replied somewhat hesitantly as she stared at me. "For a moment there, I thought it was Quan Yin walking through the door!"

"No, just plain old me," I joked.

"Yeah, right," she replied.

For the rest of the day, she continued to peek at me off and on until I laughingly told her that it was truly me she was seeing.

There are many aspects of Quan Yin all over the world, and many are powerful channels of her energy. I did not realize how powerful until I met another person who had been channeling Quan Yin for a while.

I was at a seminar and the Quan Yin Channel was presented that evening. I stood up to ask what message the channel had for me. What happened next was breathtaking. She came to me, took my hands and kissed them. Tears filled both our eyes as recognition flashed between us. At that very moment, a burst of energy radiated from both of us and filled the room. I could hear the gasps of astonishment behind me as many felt the Quan Yin energy touch their hearts. Later one lady looked at me in wonder and said, "What did you do? I have never felt such an awesome energy wave."

Another extraordinary validation of Quan Yin's presence was especially meaningful for me when it came through a child. Lakotawin and I were visiting a family with two small children one day. I developed an immediate rapport with the four year old boy. The child's verbal skills were limited because his development was slightly delayed due to a traumatic incident in his life. I had been entertaining him with songs earlier in the day, when he sat quietly on my lap playing with my Quan Yin pendant. I told him that it was a pretty lady. Lakotawin and another guest were sitting across from me and I began to divert my attention from the child to listen to their conversation. Suddenly in a clear angelic voice, the child said, "Kan Yin, Kan Yin." We were all stunned. For a magical instant, we felt Quan Yin's loving energy vibrate throughout the room.

Holding the Gateway energy, the Goddess would frequently pull me in to hold this doorway open. Again some people have the ability to bear witness to this and such was the case of a gifted young man I met at another seminar. He came to me during a break and said, "I saw you standing in the golden gate with Quan Yin. What a big job you have."

I did not and do not consider myself to be anyone special; to me it was just an assignment I had volunteered to do. It became a frequent joke between Lakotawin and myself that we both must be out of our minds to continually volunteer for challenging jobs lifetime after lifetime!

The Four Winds

I became aware after a while that Quan Yin had company. I sensed different energies, all of female vibration. One I knew, for she was already with me, staying in the background, and that was the Earth Mother, Gaia. The others I was beginning to recognize and another massage therapist confirmed their presence one day. "Who are these Goddesses around you? I know Quan Yin is always around you, but there are more now."

I asked her to describe them to me but she was only able to see one clearly. "The one sitting on your heart chakra is dressed in a gorgeous gown of red, orange and gold. Who is she?"

They finally revealed themselves in another profound vision. It was nighttime and yet it was not dark. I was on a beach somewhere for I could hear the soft sound of the lapping waves. The sky was full of blinking stars and I sensed that I was to go to a huge rock outcropping on the water's edge. There was a fire roaring in the center of this huge slab of rock. As I came closer, I noticed three women standing by the fire. They were stunning!

Two, I immediately recognized. One, of course, was Quan Yin, with her long black hair flowing from a bun and dressed in a blue/white brocade ceremonial Chinese gown. The other was Gaia, the Earth Mother. She was dressed in a flowing gauze-like green gown. It was a type of living velour but translucent, with flowers blooming off and on. She had auburn/brown hair with highlights. That was the only way I can describe the golden sheen that was in her hair. I had met her before in many of my meditations and have felt our deep connection to each other.

The third Goddess was vibrant. She was dressed in something I could only say looked like flames in a fire. The constant rippling and flowing of the red, orange, gold and blue of the gown reminded me of a flickering campfire. Her hair was surprisingly black as well and her skin looked as if she had a very dark suntan.

She looked at me in amusement as I continued to stare at all of them in awe. "Well," she chuckled. "Can you guess who I am? You know me; you have only forgotten it." With that, she floated to me and touched my third eye.

Instantly, I saw a volcano and remembered. "Pele," I whispered.

"Pele-Kino-Aha-Nei," She introduced herself with a formal bow.

"You were told to expect us," they said, "Have you not paid attention?" they said, teasing me.

"Oh, oh," I said, wracking my brain. "What clue did I miss?" Then it hit me. "The Four Winds! Do you mean the Four Winds?"

Very rarely do I go into chat rooms on the Internet but for some reason, one night I happened to log on to a site offering free readings. There was a line already but not a long one, so I decided to join the line and typed in my name. I didn't have to wait long. The gentleman who did the reading began to type the message for me. "Where are you from. Who are you? As soon as you typed in your name, a beautiful blue light flooded my room. The only message I have for you is: 'The Four Winds.' I don't know what it means but the message is repeated over and over."

I thanked him and told him, "I understood the message." I did, for at that moment, it resonated as something I needed to know. Exactly what, I was not sure at the time.

I knew I had hit the nail on the head when all three nodded, smiling. "But what does it mean? There are only three of you."

Quan Yin pointed towards me and said, "Look behind you."

My mouth must have been open for a long time for it felt dry when I came back into awareness. Elevated behind me was a female figure. I could not see her face but I knew that she was awesome. Out of her heart and stomach area flowed dazzling rays of white light that moved like lightning bolts all around her.

She almost looked like a giant Spiderwoman. "Welcome Mother, welcome Shekinah," whispered three soft voices behind me.

"I am the Mother God, the Divine Feminine, the Creation Part of God the Father."

The words were projected directly in my head, and I knew that it came from this wondrous entity. She continued, "We come to you as the Four Winds of Change, the Four Directions of Balance and the Four Elements of Creation. Each will be revealed to you in good time. We are pleased that you have answered the calling. You are to gather the feminine vessels. For the awakened female human is playing a vital role in the Earth's ability to break through the lower vibrations and join her sisters in the higher realms of Love. We will walk with you, for our beloved daughter Quan Yin has awakened her aspect within you."

I woke up shaking, not in a bad way but shaking nonetheless. The first thought that reverberated in my head was: *What on earth have I volunteered for this time?*

Suddenly information flooded through me that had me shaking my head in wonder. The Indian Shamans from South America knew the Goddess Shekina and had depicted her as Spider Woman in their ancient records. I gathered that to this day, spiders are considered sacred animals in that area. The next exciting item was when Kryon revealed the Hebrew name of the ninth DNA strand as 'Shekinah Esh - The Flame of Expansion.' The word Shekina in Hebrew is another word for God.

I was not sure what the Goddesses had in mind and decided to leave it up to them. My relationship with Quan Yin was the most comfortable for me at this point, and she gave me a little song to sing as I was driving down the highway one morning. It was amusing since there was no way I could write down the words that danced in my head. I did not want to pull over and I begged her to repeat the song once I got home. I could still hear her chuckles; she finds our lives very amusing at times.

She told me to teach it to others and use the song for healing. The song itself will bring the message into the awareness of those who are willing to open their hearts to it. Here are the words and it is to be sung three times in harmony when possible.

I am joy

I am happiness

I am Love and peacefulness

I am Light shining day and night

It brought forth the most marvelous reactions! When I taught and sang it to the group, it brought tears to their eyes. We began using it as part of a healing session and stood in a circle around the person receiving the healing energies and sang the song. The results were phenomenal. It raised the vibration of the whole room and when the person is in a state of acceptance, he/she can feel the love energies permeating into the auric field.

The Four Directions

I introduced Lakotawin earlier, and will now expand on her part in my story. Lakotawin taught me the native honoring of the Four Directions, and I began to understand this part of Shekina's message. In exchange, she asked me teach her Reiki healing and to share with her the messages regarding the New Energies.

According to Native teachings, each lodge is held differently based on the Shaman's teachings. Lakotawin conducts a bear lodge and what I share here is therefore based on that particular tradition. She invited me to join her in numerous sweat lodge ceremonies and our journey accelerated as we entered the realms of the Spirit Grandmothers and Grandfathers.

Each doorway into the Spirit world is represented in the lodge as the Four Directions – East, West, North and South. The South is guarded by the Eagle, the North by the Bear and the West by the Grandmother Spirit (the Divine Feminine), while the Creator Energy (Father God) itself holds the East.

Lakotawin would assign each participant a specific place to sit according to the messages she received just before the ceremony. She explained that based on old traditions the males would always be seated on the East side and the females on the West. The Shaman, in this case herself, occupies the North with the Fire-keeper in the Southern Doorway, which is the only entrance in or out of the lodge.

As she joined me in the knowledge of the New Energy and chose to walk the ascension path, the energy of the lodge began to shift and change as well. It manifested in an explosion of light in the center of the lodge, which is considered to be the connecting point of the Earth Mother to the Creator. We were privileged to witness a stunning display of Spiraling Lights that burst forth from a glowing lotus of light in the center during an intense sweat.

Sometimes there were people who, for their own private reasons, chose not to go in the lodge but to stay outside in a meditative state. They would still have the energetic benefits and would often witness visions while sitting outside the lodge. On one such occasion, they 'saw' lights exploding out of the lodge like a fireworks display. We realized that the vibration of the lodge had risen in accordance with the work we had done in raising our own frequencies.

It was an exciting beginning of the Great Shift, for Lakotawin began receiving energetic transmissions that prompted her to initiate the changes. She understood the implications of her decision, for she had to move against some of the old traditions. She began by negating the male and female sections, with the understanding that we are one and moving out of Duality in the higher vibrations. She knew the old customs and ceremonies were still in play, but the vibration needs to be raised in balance with the new energy.

Think of it as getting a new TV set with all the new technology in it. Now you need to find a different channel to watch your favorite old movies. On top of that, you realize that your old shows still tell the same stories but now they have been revised, improved with new actors and new special effects. Same story but what a different picture it now is.

There were still some challenges, however, for she found that not many females were able to hold the Creator doorway. The women who were put there ended up getting ill afterwards – not seriously, but just a feeling of discomfort and a major headache. Up to this point, she had positioned me in the West, the doorway of the Grandmothers. She was very happy one night when I was able to hold the door to facilitate communication with her beloved Grandmother who had passed into Spirit.

Then one day, she received the instruction to seat me in the Eastern Doorway. I felt the extraordinary strength of this door and amazingly did not get sick. I have held that doorway at every ceremony I have participated in ever since. I could feel the Creator energies flow through me, and through this strong doorway, the Divine Feminine Energies were able to communicate their messages to us. I realized that the Quan Yin Gate part of me was the one capable of holding this door open.

The Four Elements

I discussed my connection with Water earlier and had come to understand the connection to Air with the gifts of feathers that came my way. I recalled a strange observation one of my earlier teachers had, which at the time I thought very odd. "You will hear the winds speak and once you master the art of listening in the silence, you will be able to communicate with the Air around you." This message resurfaced when I discovered my connection with the winged guardians of the Air.

The presence of the third element, Earth, was evident since my childhood. It was natural for me to root and dig in the dirt, planting seedlings and cuttings at a very early age. My mother tolerated this part of me with resignation, as I would bring home all kinds of plants and seeds from my excursions and would plant them in the small patch of soil around the house. Throughout my life, I was happiest working in the garden and would create one wherever I lived. I loved the trees around me and remembered the sadness and reluctance I felt every time we had to leave our camp in the woods. This earth awareness was strengthened once I learned about Gaia, the Earth Mother. Being human, I would ask for validation repeatedly and Spirit patiently obliged each time.

The first validation came from a lady who was also very connected to the Earth energies. She happened to touch me as part of an exercise during a spiritual workshop. I remember her warm touch on my shoulders as she kept her hands there for a long time. After the session, she told me she had a message for me. "The Earth itself recognizes you. Where your feet touch the Earth, tendrils of light seem to grow out of the ground itself," she whispered in my ear. "Gaia knows who you are."

The other message was shared before a large audience during a question period: "You are strongly grounded and connected to the Earth herself. You have been one with her before and have rekindled this bond again."

It was amusing to witness the effect this message had on other people that day. A group had an excursion planned to have an Earth ceremony on the mountain the following day, and one member asked if I could join them. Regretfully, I had to decline for I had a plane to catch.

Regarding the fourth element of Fire, I've always had a fascination for fire, and my husband would jokingly tell our friends that I was a pyromaniac. When he first met me, he was astounded that I could build a fire in a rainstorm and cook breakfast for 15 campers on a wet day. I loved building campfires and cooking on an open wood fire.

One of my closest friends will never forget her decision to join me for a walk in the woods one winter. She nervously watched as I built a small fire in the snow and proceeded to boil water for coffee. We had noticed some bear tracks and she was not happy that I insisted on brewing coffee in the middle of a snowy clearing!

I introduced the Goddess Pele earlier and the fact that she is the Goddess of Fire. She resides in the volcanoes of the Hawaiian Islands, meaning that her energies are the strongest there. The Hawaiian volcanoes are the mountain peaks that remain from the ancient land of Lemuria, which is why the energies are so powerful there. The moment I set foot on the big island of Hawaii, I felt as if I'd returned home, as though a distant memory tape was being replayed.

A large group of us went to the volcano for a special ceremony conducted by one of the Hawaiian Shamans, or Kahunas. As part of the ceremony, we were to pick the berries growing around the rim of the volcano to use as an offering.

The Hawaiian people consider these 'Pele's berries,' for they are the first ones to grow after a volcanic eruption. For some reason, I kept collecting these berries after the ceremony and eating them. I was warned that it might cause diarrhea if I ate too many but, thank goodness, that never happened.

Lakotawin, who was there as well, stood at the edge of the rim and started chanting a ceremonial song called a 'water song.' She shared with me later that Pele had asked her to sing it. The song projected me out of my body and I found myself floating towards the center of the volcano. There, framed by the cloudy fumes, was Pele, magnificent in her flaming robes. She called to me and re-established our connection within the fire of the volcano. She told me, "Help others to ignite the Kundalini fires within themselves. It is important to breathe in the air deeply and to fan the ball of fire in the stomach area. It is the combining, the joining of all the elements that will eventually raise the vibration and sustain the momentum of the shift."

Pele then reminded me to remember the clue she put in my name as well. Sanscrit is an ancient language that is still used in chants and prayers and my name 'jinna' means 'Firespirit' in this language. Thus the Fire Goddess has awakened her aspect within me. My spine would frequently feel as if it has burst into a flaming torch and it is impossible for me to even lay on my back then.

The Four Winds have now been joined by the Four Directions and the Four Elements in my field. I am not quite sure what else is in store for me and to what extent my partnership with the Goddesses will grow into, but I have every intention of enjoying every moment of this adventure.

Chapter Fourteen

Animal Guides

T he first time I was made aware of animal guides was during one of my earliest attempts at forming a meditation circle. As I said earlier, there was a huge spirit eagle hovering above us that night. Through Lakotawin's teachings, I become more aware of these special energies and I thanked each one who entered my field with their loving gifts.

The Eagle

The Eagle was the first strong manifestation of energy as I continued my journey. During numerous sweat lodges, it became more apparent that I had a deep affinity with the Eagle energy. I received a number of etheric feathers during these manifestations in the lodge. I watched with fascination as I saw the Eagle take a feather from its wing and then present it to me.

The Eagle that came to me was the Bald Eagle, and I came to understand that this energy is strongly associated with that of water energy. It was the perfect strand that connected the elements of air and water.

It also brought in:

- The illumination of Spirit
- Healing energy
- Awakening of psychic ability
- Awakening the ability to walk between worlds[1]

It began to make sense, for I could hear the clicking sounds as each piece fell in place. I was eventually gifted with a physical eagle feather.

The Red-tailed Hawk

My next winged guardian came from Lakotawin's husband, The Big Raven. He was an Elder and quite ill when I met him. He had asked for a healer to help him and was shown a vision of a woman with black hair. Lakotahwin only knew about this when he told us that, and when I walked towards him, he immediately recognized me as her. As a token of his gratitude, he presented me with the red-tailed hawk's wing feather and shared with me that his visions told him I carried the Hawk energy.

The Red-tailed Hawk is another powerful animal totem and brings the following vibration to the one who resonates with this frequency:

- Guardian and protector of the Air
- Visionary power
- Key to higher levels of consciousness
- A teacher of higher expressions of psychism and visions
- Awakened Kundalini energy
- Moving into Awareness of Soul Purpose[2]

---

[1] *Animal Speaks* by Ted Andrews
[2] ibid

When this totem appears, it is a sign that there is an important message coming your way, so you need to pay attention. It also is the sign that the time is right for your childhood dreams and visions to be fulfilled. This Hawk has the ability to soar very high in the sky and is the symbol of the potential to soar in your passion and creativity. However, it is also a bird of prey and has the power to attack and hurt anyone who hinders its flight. For the bearer of this totem, it is therefore important to be fully aware of this instinctive reaction when blocked from reaching your highest potentials. The people of the Pueblo also call this particular hawk 'the Red Eagle,' and consider it to be just as powerful a sacred totem.

This trail continued with the gift of another feather many months later. A friend who was an avid golfer was golfing in Florida that winter and came back with this story. He was standing below a tree on the golf course and noticed a red-tailed hawk sitting on a branch. The hawk made a sound and then proceeded to pluck a feather from its wing. It then told my friend to bring the feather to me. What a message that was and what a gift.

I did not realize how strong the presence of this energy was in my field until a year later when Lakotahwin and I went to visit her Indian friends in New York State. When we arrived at the house, I was stunned to see a wild red-tailed hawk in a big wire cage in the yard. The couple who lived here had rescued the injured hawk and were nursing it back to health. It was a very moving moment for me to be able to communicate with this vibrant energy at such close quarters. Before I left, I was gifted with a magnificent red tail feather of the hawk and a small ceremonial prayer stick decorated with numerous hawk feathers. I felt very honored by the unique present.

Beside the hawk cage there was also an owl that our friends had rescued and I learned that the Owl is the Night energy equivalent to the Hawk's Daytime energy. The Owl with the Hawk together is a strong totem to help balance the male and the female energies. My visit was very educational and I was very grateful for the teachings that this beautiful couple gave me.

The Bear

The Bear had by this time also made its presence known. Upon entering my driveway, a visitor was startled one morning when he thought he saw a huge bear standing before my house.

Since Lakotawin conducts a Bear-lodge, the Bear totem plays a very important role both in her life and in mine. It is a very strong symbol and brings forth The Awakening of the Power of the Unconscious. According to Native lore, Bear medicine will teach you to go deep within yourself, and tap into the deep well of inner knowingness that will help you make your choices.

The Bear is also considered a sign for Healers, and a major protector of the people.

The Turtle

The next animal was an unexpected surprise – the turtle – an animal that lives both on land and in water. Here is another connection of the elements, for where the eagle connects the Air to the Water, the turtle is the strand that connects the Earth to the Water. The turtle is an ancient creature and the energy of this totem is of Motherhood, a symbol of the primal mother energies of Longevity and Awakening to Opportunities.

It brings back something a friend of mine said to me at the early stages of my path. "You carry the energy of the eternal mother, one who mothers all." I have always thought that he was commenting on my concern for my daughter, who was ill at the time. It made sense now, especially after having experienced a number of my other lives where I seem to play the role of Mother again and again. Many see me as a very old soul and sometimes I feel like a very tired one!

In ancient mythology, the turtle shell was a symbol for heaven and its underside that of Earth. When you have this energy, it can help you create heaven on earth within your own lifetime. Isn't this what the new energies are all about?

Turtle medicine stimulates the gifts of clairaudience and clairvoyance. It awakens the higher senses and it is also a reminder to slow down our hectic lives. A turtle is never in a hurry. It also represents a very grounding symbol, a strong connection to the earth energies. For those who feel the ground shifting underneath you, call on the Turtle energy for it will ground and stabilize your base.

It made its presence known by presenting me with gifts. It began with a friend of mine who dropped by and brought me a beautiful large painting of a turtle by a native Australian artist. Then during my visit in Hawaii, a very intuitive lady brought me the message that I carried the Turtle energy. Gifts truly rained on me from that moment on. Turtle earrings, turtle carvings, sand turtles, and a turtle pendant. So many, in fact, that it became quite amusing.

Chapter Fifteen

Completion

Phantom Death

The Phantom Death experience is an unavoidable part of the Path of the Great Shift for those who choose to walk it. The decision to enter the transformation is oftentimes made at the subconscious level, and the conscious mind is not fully aware of it at first. The intensity of each experience varies according to the individual person and it is not easily detected.

This was the case with me, and I went into it with the clumsiness of a novice. The Phantom Death is the death of the old self, and it can be just as traumatic an experience as a real death situation. For some, it can happen more than once, as I found out in the later stages of my passage into the higher frequencies.

My first initiation into this phenomenon was the one that jarred me into awakening and started me off on my spiritual quest. I went through it relatively quickly for a first timer, for it took me only about a week to realize that I had changed drastically. I went through the whole gamut of emotional trauma during that first exposure. Not understanding what I was going through at that time, it was a taxing experience.

First I felt as if I was turned inside out, as I screamed and sobbed my way through the unfamiliar flood of emotions. It really felt as if parts of me were dying, and I wanted to die and move into the actual death sequence. I had physical pain as well, and my body felt disengaged, detached, as I traveled through the layers of anger and denial followed by the grieving state. Then came the final stages of acceptance and surrender. At that point, I entered the stillness, a void, a state of no being, of waiting for something elusive I could not fathom what it was.

The change was very subtle and yet very dramatic at the same time. I felt discombobulated, a sensation of not belonging anywhere, and of severance from everything familiar. I went through my chores but was functioning on automatic and couldn't remember much of what I had done or not done.

The hours became days and the days flowed into a week. Then, suddenly, I looked up and out of myself, surprised at what I saw. The calibration and adjustment period would continue for some time, but that initial awareness was like the first day of spring. Everything seemed strange, dissimilar, and even my body felt changed. My aches and pains began to subside, and my zest for living was renewed. The sky and the earth looked different, everything looked brighter and more vibrant, like a sunny day after a cleansing shower. My attitudes and my relationships with other people had also changed. Situations that used to bother me were now strangely unimportant.

My family stepped gingerly around this new me, uncertain about how to relate to this stranger. Patiently I would assure them that I loved them dearly and that I was still there for them but in a different way. My friends were also surprised and immediately wondered what had happened to cause this radical change.

Through my studies and investigations into this phenomenon, I learned that I had gone through a fast forward process of a mini-reincarnation sequence. The old me had vacated the premises, and a new me entered immediately into the same body. It required a large amount of energy to go through this procedure, and it has been made possible for everyone since the arrival of the stronger elevated energies.

The spirit-self can leave the body completely and the life-force energy will maintain the physical body for a very long time, sometimes months before it enters the deterioration process. This is a difficult concept for many including myself, and it took many hours of going within to gain the understanding and acceptance of it. This brings more clarity to the puzzling areas of near-death experiences where the body seems to come back to life after being pronounced deceased.

The second time it occurred was a complete shock, for it came in extremely fast and lasted only about an hour. I knew immediately what was happening this time, but it still threw me into an uncomfortable situation. I was in a roomful of people in the process of completing a weeklong teacher's training course.

I had been feeling at odds with myself for three days prior and thought it was just fatigue, for the course was very intense. On that last day, I found myself withdrawing, not wishing to interact and sought solitude in a corner. Abruptly, I began the cycle of crying and sobbing. I could not stop, as wave upon wave of the same feeling of disengaging enveloped me. At that moment, it felt so right for me to leave. I knew I had completed all the contracts I'd scripted for this lifetime, and there was no compulsion to stay any longer.

Knowing what was happening did not lessen the grief of separation, the act of mourning, as if I was saying good-bye to my present life. I could hear myself saying over and over, "It feels so right this time. I am done."

Grace, my friend, sensed the change in me and came rushing in. She took one look and knew what was going on. She said, "Don't you dare go now. We need you here more than the other side."

What was different this time was that another friend was going through it at the same time. We ended up huddled together, holding on to each other as we cried it out. Those who recognized what we were going through came and held our hands or just sat beside us, holding a safe healing space for us. In retrospect, I think the very high group energy in the room propelled us through the process at an incredible speed.

Then suddenly, it was over, as if someone just turned a tap off. The crying stopped, the tears were gone. The peace, the stillness and a sense of completion surrounded me once again. I had chosen to return and a new me had reentered. I welcomed her gratefully, for I perceived this as a sign that my journey had intensified, accelerated and the old me was getting a well-deserved rest.

The third exit point was even faster and more forceful. It happened during a powerful sweat lodge ceremony where four other women of high vibration joined me. All five of us were in Hawaii together and had a strong connection to the Goddess Pele. Their combined energies supported the opportunity for another shift for me.

Again I dissolved into sobs and heart-wrenching tears. The feeling of entering the perfect moment to depart encircled my body and the sense of separation was very potent. My friends were very supportive and knew I had to make this difficult decision on my own every time. They gave me permission to leave but at the same time, they made sure I knew how much they loved me. Propelled by their wish to have me around a bit longer, they also reminded me of the new contracts I had already agreed to.

They were right. I had unconsciously put my feet in a new stream of agreements to help and therefore the option to continue my work on Earth, as difficult as it was, was set in place. However the sense of completion and of detachment with everything I had known so far became a sound argument for not staying, and the choice was still mine to make. On the other hand, I had been given an astonishing gift a few weeks prior to this event and it had helped me reach a greater comprehension about the whole procedure. It swayed my choice.

An entity called Raven channeled by Rev. Fred Sterling had diverted my question with the following statement: "You know you have completed what you came to do here on Earth. All choices are honored and if you choose to go, we will personally carry you on our backs and fly you home. However we hope that you will choose to stay because you are much needed here."

This surprise tribute had touched me deeply and reminded me of the familiar phrase, "Three strikes and you're out." 'Out' this time for me would mean out of the loop of the phantom death cycles as I made my final choice. I realized that my multi-layered Being at a higher level had already made the selection and that the awareness of it was just beginning to seep through to my conscious self. I agreed to stay to fulfill my wish to witness the miraculous shift happening on the Earth plane right now.

This time I truly gave myself permission to create new contracts at a higher level with any relationships I chose to enter as I continued my journey. I had completed my assignments and there were no more specific paths for me to follow. There was no longer any need to have defined exit points, for I had gained the knowledge and the ability of vacating my human shell at any time during this new lifespan on Earth.

Numerology

I do not know much about numerology and can only share what I have learned thus far. It is becoming more and more apparent that numbers play a very vital role in the process of creation. When understood, number energy can be a great tool for us to use. The interest in quantum physics is rising as our collective awareness begins to expand, and scientists have begun to realize the presence of a spiritual component within higher mathematical equations.

Our Merkabah or etheric light body, for example, is an intricate structure of many geometric shapes of light and this mathematical configuration is known as Sacred Geometry. The Fibonacci number sequence[1] is another fascinating model of the spiritual connection to Higher Mathematical concepts, for it is found in the physical world all around us.

For us average people, it is just a fun and interesting thing to see how numbers affect our lives. Some numbers keep their representation regardless of what they are used for but some have different meanings for different subjects. For example, take the day, month and year of your birth, and add up the numbers until you have only a one-digit number (with the exception of the master numbers, such as 11 and 12).

The number 9 for instance is considered a sign for completion. Whether you are looking at your life lessons or the number for your name or any other areas of your life, it usually stands for a finishing point,

I was not aware of its clues until a friend of mine who was into numerology commented on it. My name adds up to a nine, my birth date plus year is a nine, I live on lot number nine, my

---

[1]   The series begins with 0, 1, 2, with each successive number being the sum of the two previous numbers, giving the sequence 0, 1, 2, 3, 5, 8, 13, 21, 34, 55, 89, 144, 233, 377, 610, etc.

license plate numbers add up to nine, and the four digits of my phone number add up to nine. The message of completion had been staring me in the face all along!

The year 2007 is a nine and there is a potential of a great shift in consciousness on September 18th that year. It makes for an exciting anticipation of a major changing event if this potential continues its movement towards manifestation. The Divine Feminine Light energy will then be fully anchored within the Earth itself, initiating a faster rise in frequency, bolstering a momentum we all have been waiting for. Looking at my numerology then, I will have three nines that month, nine for the year, nine for my birthday (September 18 = 9 + 9 = 18 = 9) and my age on that day also adds up to a nine.

With these unbelievable coincidences, I could not deny my destiny any longer. After all, what are the odds of having exactly 3 nines on that precise date? I have no leg to stand on and could not argue against it even if I tried.

According to Archangel Michael, '999' stands for the three levels of the trinity of Completion. What a colossal message this is for me!

Chrysalis

We are in a momentous time right now, and are the lucky ones who are able to get front row seats! What a privilege to be alive today and be a part of this 'Shift of the Ages' that will affect the whole Universe itself. This was another persuasive argument that drew me back into this fascinating lifetime.

This existence as we know it is slowly disappearing as the altering vibrations increase in frequency. We are about to make a gigantic leap in human evolution, raising and expanding our level of consciousness. I touched this area lightly in the beginning of my story and would like to discuss it a bit further.

To be able to enter or even survive in the higher vibrations, we cannot take the lower vibrations with us. In other words, we cannot take any baggage on this spectacular excursion. The heavier vibrations are functioning at a much lower frequency and cannot exist in the higher dimensions. Remember the electrical wiring of an old house; it cannot withstand the surge of a new power grid. Or if you brought a hair dryer from England, where the electrical system runs at 50 Hz, and plugged it in over here, it would run faster and soon wear itself out or even blow up. Another example is ice. It cannot exist in water for long until it melts, and only then can it flow easily but it cannot rise. It will have to change again into vapor before it can rise and become one with the air. Ice is the heaviest and its molecules vibrate slowly until it begins to melt. Then the molecules vibrate faster as it turns into liquid and faster still when it becomes vapor.

In the same fashion, our bodies need to transform from a denser structure to a lighter one. To achieve this, we must release all of the heavy compacted energies we have accumulated throughout our lifetimes. Most of us recognize these heavy energies as our dark side or shadow self. We cannot deny this part of ourselves, even though we have tried to hide it, and shove it under the carpet. It has carried all our heavy luggage of negative emotions, thought patterns and actions for a very long time. This shadow self is tired now and seeks resolution; it does not want the job any longer. We must not forget that the Ego is also a vital part of this shadowy partnership.

On one side is the denial of the existence of Light which plunges one into complete darkness or the complete absence of Light, labeled by humans as 'evil.' The far side of this is just as imbalanced for it is the complete denial of the darkness or shadow-self and there is only acceptance of Light. This imbalance is not always recognized, especially by Lightworkers with the perception that anything to do with the shadow-self is wrong. I was puzzled at first when I saw this happening with some persons who consider themselves fully on the path of enlightenment. My observations and information regarding this state revealed an existence of being constantly ungrounded, frequent inability to make practical life choices and a sense of compassion that lacks depth. It also creates a 'cotton-candy' type of thinking that often makes it difficult to have a meaningful conversation with the person. I also observed that someone who has chosen to experience this imbalance has difficulty completing assignments or sometimes even keeping a job. The Ego-self is just as strongly anchored here as it is within the Shadow imbalance. On one side, there is too much heaviness of compacted energies and on the other side, there is too much lightness and thus no grounding connection.

The object thus is to move out of the imbalanced energies of duality (male/female, dark/light) into the balanced energy where both the Light-self and Shadow-self dance in Oneness and Divine Love for each other. I think of it as a painting. White paint on a white canvas will barely show anything but when the artist creates a picture by blending the light and dark colors together, what a fantastic balanced composition it then becomes. Another way to look at it is in connection with food. When I cook a dish, I know I need to balance all the herbs to create a delicious meal. Too much sugar or too much salt will not be pleasing to any palate.

A more graphic example would be the life cycle of a caterpillar. It needs to isolate itself in a cocoon before it can transform into the butterfly. To assist us with our perception, we can take this process of chrysalis as an analogy to illustrate our journey towards enlightenment. Before the caterpillar can even begin to grow its wings, it must let go of its former body completely.

It literally melts down to its molecular DNA structure. Graphically, it begins to liquefy itself; in other words it has a phantom death. Once this has been accomplished, this liquid life force then begins to restructure and rebuild a whole new body, a body that now can fly and is no longer restricted to crawling on a leaf. The basic molecular components of this butterfly are still the same as that of the caterpillar, but its essence has now transformed into a higher vibration of being that can fly with two colorful wings in complete balance, joined as one with a new body.

Cocoon

Drawing a line of comparison from the caterpillar's life, we can easily see what we need to do. The cocoon is a perfect analogy of the stillness of meditation, of going within that is crucial to our journey into transformation. Within the denser environment, we used to reach out of ourselves for the answers. We searched for the right teachers, the right gurus and often followed the popular choices of the masses. With the higher voltage of the new energy, this method to reach enlightenment is no longer in play. There is no need for a guru any longer, for G (gee) U(you) R(are) U(you).

The answers we seek are and have been inside our hearts all along. We have just forgotten the access code to that program. Upon our request, angelic helpers have come to assist us to remember so that we can begin to re-teach ourselves how to use the new software with a new power surge.

My restful time at the cottage was my time of entering the cocoon state. The retreat from the hassles and temptations of the old life was the weaving of my cocoon of silence. I lost interest in TV or radio, I didn't know what had happened on 9/11 until a friend of mine called to talk about it. I relished the void around me and felt deprived every time I had to leave it.

My most treasured memories were of solitary walks in the woods during the day and meandering along the lanes on snowy full moon nights.

I felt completely at peace in my isolation and was astounded when a friend stopped by one day to tell me about her puzzling dream. "I had a strange vision-like dream last night. I was told that I was to keep watch over you and to protect you. I was dressed in armor, like an ancient knight, and you were in this huge golden cocoon. Does this make sense to you?"

The remarkable part was that this wonderful person was an officer in the armed forces, who happened to be stationed in this area. My eyes were full of grateful tears as I explained to her what the energies of transformation were all about. Her eyes were teary as well as she continued, "I'm standing beside your cocoon, holding a sword with shining jewels and strange symbols on the silver hilt. I will stand guard as long as you need me." This human guardian angel was transferred out of the area two years later. My deep gratitude and love will surround her where ever she may be.

The disintegrating part was the toughest and most challenging aspect of the procedure. The phantom death phenomena definitely played a major role in this liquefying process of the cocoon state. I honestly felt as if I was wrapped in a type of shell, for I had no interest at all in doing anything that involved loud noises or places with crowds. Going to the mall became uncomfortable, which was unusual for a person who used to love shopping in malls. This was a long process in the journey and a huge challenge for many of us, especially if you don't know what you're going through.

I had to release my whole belief system, everything that I had been taught by my parents and various teachers. It was as if I was dealing with an addiction and trying to get off the vicious spiral. The multitudes of behavior patterns, habits, attitudes and thought patterns were next. It was a struggle to even recognize each one, and then a lot of effort unraveling and dissolving these heavy tendencies. Control and judgment issues, followed by drama, were big items on my list of disintegrating. Being a Virgo, I did not 'see' my controlling nature and my insistence on perfection and order in my daily life. Expectations of outcome and planning of agendas were rooted deeply within my teacher's aspect, and to let that go took a lot of soul searching.

No one can do this alone and I faced this fact with resignation, for accepting help from anyone was one of my heavier attributes.

I realized that I could not see my face unless I look into a mirror, so I need others to hold the mirrors to help me. Imagine walking into one of those rooms full of different mirrors at an amusement park and seeing different reflections of you.

Unfortunately, human mirrors are not as much fun, for they are the people you interact with every day. At a subconscious level, each person reflects the congestion you need to see and it works both ways. To illustrate this, look at the number of drivers getting agitated every time another car cuts them off or follows them too closely. They start yelling obscenities and sometimes even use rude gestures to relate their anger to the other driver.

What I find amusing is that the other driver cannot hear this tirade and often is not aware of it. That being the case, who is the angry driver's audience? Who is actually hearing his voice?

Many women have told me about their embarrassment when their husbands react this way in traffic. I would help them to understand that, first of all, there's no reason to be embarrassed since it was not their behavior pattern. There's no need to pick up another person's load unless you insist on carrying it on your back. Secondly, his brain does not compute the fact that he will face similar incidences until he recognizes his own anger. The other driver is just a mirror, showing him what he needs to 'see' in himself.

Road rage is just an expanded mirror, getting bigger and bigger, until drivers begin to realize that the anger and violent reactions originate from within themselves. The words they are spouting are directed at themselves and no other. Words, thoughts and actions are powerful energies that have the qualities of a boomerang. It will always come back to the one who throws it.

Rebirth

The chakra system in our bodies holds the code that triggers the evolution into a new being. The heavy congestion of energy in the chakras form a blockade that stops the life force energy line from flowing freely and keeping all the layers of the body healthy. All seven chakras are anchored in the spine, which is like a main electrical panel in a house. Once the line is cleared, full power is restored and every 'bulb' in the Lightbody can now be activated.

A healthy chakra spins like a fan and, like a fan, will spin slower if the blades are not clean. Each emotional release increases the speed of the spin, causing its light to brighten. Eventually when all seven chakras are spinning freely, the flow of Light increases in the energy tube located in the spine. The Kundalini energy can now rise without hindrance, purifying and rebalancing the system.

Soon another dream vision substantiated my version of Chrysalis. I saw my cocoon cracking like an egg. I was still inside, lying in fetal position. It looked like a repeat of the same scene as the one at the very beginning of my journey, except that there was a sense of anticipation here. The next frame found me lying on my side outside the cocoon, wet as if I had had a shower with two soggy towels covering my back. For some reason, I felt exhausted and just wanted to lie there to rest. Wonderful warmth radiated from the golden sun above and a balmy caressing breeze rapidly dried up all the moisture on me.

Feelings of wonder, surprise and overwhelming joy welled up as I found myself standing in the sunlight with beautiful shimmering, colorful wings on my back. Soft whispers spiraled in the wind and, looking up, I saw a multitude of exquisite winged beings flying, gliding and floating against the backdrop of an azure blue sky. They sang and called to me. To this day, I have no words to describe the emotional high I felt as I joined them in flight.

Not long after, a wonderful friend and human angel gave me a gift. She put a small box in my hand and said, "I was guided to buy this pretty butterfly brooch not knowing who it was for until I saw you."

As I said earlier, there is no longer any need for me to follow a road map. Like the butterfly, I can now fly in any direction I choose, land on any pathway where I can help another traveler, whenever they invite me to their side. I have accepted and embraced every part of me, both my shadow-self and my light-self. I accept only the wisdom of each experience, light or dark, and offer it with compassion and understanding to any traveler I meet on my path. My mission statement has not changed; it is still the same: "I am of service to all, including myself, for ultimately we are all ONE, and Divine LOVE is all that matters."

I do not claim to know all the answers, for my answers are customized for me. I hope that my personal story can be of assistance for any seekers along the enlightenment path, and that each will find their own answers within.

The Gift of the Lotus

The lotus seed, a tiny cocoon, fell and drifted down into a pond. Alone, it descended into the murky depths, full of hazards. It was buffeted by the rough waves and not treated very kindly by the aquatic life all around as it sank further to the bottom. Sharp rocks gouged its shell, fish tried to take a bite of it and it finally reached a safe haven – a patch of mud. Sand and debris settled over and around it forming yet another cocoon.

In this deep, dark stillness, a memory began to stir and the seed remembered. It grew roots to anchor it deep into the rocks and soil below. The roots became as one with the Earth and the Earth supplied it with nutrients to create a stalk. The stalk knew that it had to become one with the water, or it would be damaged and break. So the stalk swayed and danced with the water as it grew upwards, seeking the light high above. Finally it broke through the surface and brought forth its leaves. The leaves unfurled themselves and felt the air and the warm rays of the sun. They knew they had to become one with the air and the heat of the sun to transform nutrients into green chlorophyll to feed and nourish the whole plant. And so they did.

The plant rejoiced and a tiny bud poked its head and wormed its way between the floating leaves reaching for the light. With a grateful sigh, the bud stretched itself and burst open, freeing its pearlescent petals of pink and white. The lotus blossom opened its heart and displayed its beauty. The water formed a loving cradle as it rocked the lotus in the gentle breeze, while greeted by the golden rays of a new day.

The lotus has emerged.

About the Author

Jinna is a retired school teacher who was born off the East coast of Sumatra in Indonesia. She has made her home in Canada since 1967 and lives with her husband in a small community in Northern Ontario.

Jinna is a twice-ordained Minister. She is a metaphysical minister ordained by Lightworker and a spiritual minister registered under the International Assembly of Spiritual Healers.

She is a Reiki Master and certified in numerous energy healing modalities such as EMF, IET, Healing Touch and Acu-Touch. She is a certified aromatherapist and also a certified instructor for the Lightworker Spiritual Psychology course. She continues to offer many classes and workshops in her home or where ever she is invited to do so.

Jinna is also the Founder of the New Energy Healing modality coined EHF (Energy Healing Facilitator) and has begun to introduce this course in numerous cities in Canada and in the United States. Teaching and learning continue to be her passion and it is a major part of her everyday life.

About the Cover Art Illustrator

Carlos Rubio is a Columbian-born multi-talented Canadian artist who, after having explored the engineering field, decided to shift direction towards the artistic stream.

He graduated as a graphic designer from Seneca College in Toronto and is currently working as a professional in this field. He continues with his passion in painting and illustration during his leisure time. He has produced a number of exceptional pieces for private viewing only at this time.

Connect with spiritual family:

http:// www.Lightworker.com

'The Beacons of Light Re-minders from Home'
monthly messages from the Group, are available online or
as a free e-mail service by request.

http://www.Lightworker.com/Schedule

Connect with original spiritual family on the message boards
and in the chat rooms. Set your creations into motion in the 8
Sacred Rooms. Lightworker is a large site where the Groups information is translated into 20 languages. Come spend time creating
Home.

Re-member… You are not alone… Welcome Home

Paths to Empowerment Seminars
from Lightworker

Paths to Empowerment Seminars provide practical applications of the information for living in the higher vibrations of the new planet Earth, based on information from the Group. All gatherings include practical techniques for evolving as empowered humans, together with a Live channel from the Group through Steve Rother.

One day informational seminars

Designed to connect family and introduce a new way of thinking ad living as empowered humans.

Two day Interactive seminars

Experiential seminars over two days that apply practical applications of the material being covered. Each workshop is desdribed in greater detail on the web site.

Three day OverLight Trainings

Three days of working with one of the OverLight modalities for healers shows the applications of the specific modality. Certified trainings. Several OverLight modalities have been adapted for a three day intensive. More on the OverLight modalities including a detailed description of each can be found at http://Lightworker.com/OverLight

Six day OverLight Facilitator Trainings

Spiritual Psychology, Transition Team Training, Spiritual Communication, Human Angel Harmonics and Inverse Wave Therapy are th first of these with more added each year. The six day trainings are for those wishing to have a complete understanding of this material and its uses in daily life or for facilitators who wish to offer these modalities in their own work as facilitators. These are Lightworker certified courses.

Check the schedule on the web site at:
http://Lightworker.com/Schedule

You will receive notification of events in your area by adding your name to our mailing list at:
http://Lightworker.com/Signup

Re-member:

A Handbook for Human Evolution

This book will re-mind you how to:

- Discover and step into your 'Plan B' Contract.
- Purposefully craft your own reality and create your own version of Home on Earth.
- Adjust to the new levels of vibration affecting your biology.
- Master the arts of Time Warping and moving between Alternate Realities.
- Re-discover your gifts and tap into your own guidance and Re-member your power.
- Play "the Game" to the Highest Outcome and enjoy the journey.
- Prepare for the next phase of our evolution and the Crystal Children who are coming.

It's an exciting time on Planet Earth. In this enlightening book, Steve Rother and the Group offer a look at Higher Truths that will change the paradigms and the way we perceive ourselves. We Humans have just won the Grand Game of Hide-and-Seek and are now moving the Game to a new level!

"Mankind is evolving. We are moving from a motivation of survival to a motivation of unity. We are reaching for 'Higher Truths' in all areas as a quiet revolution is taking place. This transition does not have to be difficult. This book documents not only profound information for the planet, but also the LOVE journey of two enlightened and high-vibrational people."

— Lee Carroll, author of The Kryon Writings

"This book will remind you of why you are here on the planet at this time. Peace is real now, and Steve's work will help you find that magic place within yourself."

— James Twyman, author of Emissary of Light, The Secret of the

Spiritual Psychology

The Twelve Primary Life Lessons

Have you ever wondered why it is that one person can grow up with every conceivable advantage, and yet seem incapable of mastering even the simplest things in life?

Have you ever known someone who, despite being highly intelligent, keeps on repeating the same mistakes over and over again?

It is only when we begin to view the human experience as the evolutionary process of a soul that we can begin to understand all these strange forces at work in our lives.

We see ourselves as human beings searching for a spiritual awakening when, in fact, we are spiritual beings trying to cope with a human awakening. But what causes us to seek these experiences in the first place? What is it, precisely, that sets certain life patterns into motion? Why do these patterns emerge in our own behaviors repeatedly? More importantly, what would happen if we could find ways of identifying this higher purpose and in so doing transform seemingly destructive patterns into positive attributes?

Spiritual Psychology offers a radically different view of life and the human experience. This book offers a view of humanity from the higher perspective of our own spirit.

"This book gives us help for our bodies, sanity for our minds and food for our Souls."

       – CHARLES L. WHITFIELD, MD, author of Healing Your Inner Child and The Truth about Mental Illness

       – BARBARA HARRIS WHITFIELD, RT, author of Spiritual Awakenings

"The word 'psychology' originally meant 'study of the soul' (psyche). After exploring far afield, we are returning full circle to encompass an understanding of ourselves as spiritual beings into our understanding of human health and behavior. Steve Rother's remarkable pioneering work is a cornerstone in challenging us to expand our knowledge and skills as empowered and empowering healers."

       – PAULINE DELOZIER, Ph.D., Clinical Psychologist

Welcome Home

The New Planet Earth

Welcome to the 5th dimension. Did you feel the ascension? The world we knew is rapidly evolving. Life on planet Earth is becoming increasingly unpredictable. The old rules no longer function. According to 'the Group,' these changes have greater implications than we imagine. As unexpected as recent events have been, they merely mark the beginning. The evolution of mankind has begun.

The Group's purpose is to prepare us for what lies ahead. In Welcome Home, they otter us keys to unlocking the secrets of developing our full power as creators, and using them in our lives now.

Welcome Home is divided into four sections:

1. Current Events: A cosmic view of where we are, how we got here and where we are heading.

2. The New Planet Earth: The new attributes of life in the 5th dimension and how we can apply them right now.

3. Questions and Answers on a wide range of topics taken from live presentations.

4. Where do we go from here? Prepare to be surprised!

"Steve Rother has tapped into the root of a new consciousness blossoming in the hearts of Humanity. Re-Member offered practical step-by-step instructions on how to awaken to the Pathway of the Soul. Welcome Home is the next step ... useful, loving, wise, and beautifully engaging – another tremendous book for the 'enlightened seeker.'"

– ISHA LERNER, author of Inner Child and Power of Flower cards

"Steve and the Group present an exciting new way to look at our world. This book provides a deeper understanding of the power and miracles that are now available to us."

– Ronna Herman, author and messenger for Archangel Michael

"Did anyone notice that life has changed? Perhaps you also feel that time has sped up and the spiritual rules are getting overhauled. Are you asking the question, 'What's next?' If so, you have the right book in your hands! Join Steve, Barbara and the Group for more loving insights into one of the greatest energy shifts our planet has ever seen."

– LEE CARROLL, author of The Kryon Writings

Each month Spiritual Family Gathers for the **VirtualLight Broadcast.**

Lightworker presents a 3-hour international broadcast free of charge on the Internet to connect spiritual family on the new planet Earth.

Each month see:

Special Guests each month, leaders in Lightwork.

2 minute readings from Steve & the Group

Lightworker events and attractions.

The Beacons of Light message from the Group presented live.

Watch it live on the Internet at: http://Lightworker.com

or

Attend in person in Las Vegas, Nevada

or

Watch the shows at your convenience in their entirety at:

http://VirtualLightBroadcast.com